Another Blow for Life ...

George Godwin

Nabu Public Domain Reprints:

You are holding a reproduction of an original work published before 1923 that is in the public domain in the United States of America, and possibly other countries. You may freely copy and distribute this work as no entity (individual or corporate) has a copyright on the body of the work. This book may contain prior copyright references, and library stamps (as most of these works were scanned from library copies). These have been scanned and retained as part of the historical artifact.

This book may have occasional imperfections such as missing or blurred pages, poor pictures, errant marks, etc. that were either part of the original artifact, or were introduced by the scanning process. We believe this work is culturally important, and despite the imperfections, have elected to bring it back into print as part of our continuing commitment to the preservation of printed works worldwide. We appreciate your understanding of the imperfections in the preservation process, and hope you enjoy this valuable book.

ANOTHER BLOW FOR LIFE.

A HOME IN BETHNAL GREEN.

ANOTHER BLOW FOR LIFE.

BY GEORGE GODWIN, F.R.S.
AUTHOR OF
"LONDON SHADOWS," "TOWN SWAMPS AND SOCIAL BRIDGES," EDITOR OF "THE BUILDER,"
ETC. ETC. ETC.

ASSISTED BY MR. JOHN BROWN.

"The world may say I've fail'd; I have *not* fail'd.
If I set truth 'fore men they will not see,
'Tis they who fail, not I. My faith holds firm,
And time will prove me right."
— CHARLES SWAIN.

With Forty-One Illustrations.

LONDON:
WM. H. ALLEN & CO., 13, WATERLOO PLACE, S.W.
1864.

LONDON:
COX AND WYMAN, PRINTERS, GREAT QUEEN STREET,
LINCOLN'S INN FIELDS.

PRELIMINARY.

LATELY, the people of Great Britain have been so violently excited by death in the workroom, amongst satin and flowers, death in the mother's arms, and death in the dank cellar; by death in Regent Street, death in Clerkenwell, and death in Bethnal Green, all premature and unnecessary, that they can scarcely require many more violent impulses to lead them to take any steps that may be necessary to prevent the repetition of such horrors,—to stop the involuntary suicide and unintentional murder now daily and hourly committed in the very centres of civilization.

Some previous endeavours on the part of the writer, humble but most earnest, to make apparent the frightful condition of parts of the metropolis and other large towns; the way in which life is shortened, health depreciated, happiness prevented, how the manners are degraded, crime and sorrow increased,—to show the evils that lie hidden around us on every side, and in the suppression of which all classes are, even selfishly, concerned,—met with wide and satisfactory recognition.

These endeavours had the countenance, if the observation may be permitted, of the good and illustrious Prince whom the nation does not cease to deplore; and Her Majesty the Queen was pleased "very graciously to accept," in special terms, the little volumes setting forth some of the results of many examinations of the houses and resorts of the toiling population, made with a view to that suppression.

The evils pointed out, the dangers deplored, unhappily still remain,—modified to some extent, it may be, by the efforts of a gradually advancing public opinion, the result of increased knowledge; and I am impelled and encouraged once more to place before the public a body of observations bearing on the subject, with a statement of some definite requirements attainable without difficulty by governing powers, and some hints that may, it is hoped, be useful to those moving in a much higher sphere than the miserable dwellers in the fever-tainted dens of Bethnal Green, Whitechapel, and Spitalfields.

Ten years ago, I pointed attention to the miserable condition of these districts, and said, "From dirt comes death." The warning, however, failed to produce any appreciable effect, or the country might have been spared the ghastly recitals which, day after day, have recently filled the public journals.

All are willing to admit that evil is done by want of head as well as by want of heart; but few, even where the will is good and disposition kindly, stop to inquire how far their own head fails,—to what extent they might themselves aid in changing a state of things they know to be evil and deplore. It will be a reward if any such be brought to thought and so led to action by the statements in this little book.

GEORGE GODWIN.

BROMPTON, *December*, 1863.

CONTENTS.

CHAPTER I.
THE EAST OF LONDON... *Page* 1

CHAPTER II.
INFANTICIDE WITHOUT INTENTION................................ 17

CHAPTER III.
HIDDEN DANGERS—AN EAST-END TEA-GARDEN........................ 23

CHAPTER IV.
THE DANGERS OF OVERCROWDING.................................. 29

CHAPTER V.
ST. LUKE'S—WHETSTONE PARK—ST. CLEMENT'S DANES—WATER 47

CHAPTER VI.
THE THAMES—WORK TO BE DONE 57

CHAPTER VII.
DRURY LANE—HOUSES OF THE DANGEROUS CLASSES 63

CHAPTER VIII.
THE ITALIAN QUARTER 71

CHAPTER IX.
THE CITY ROAD: NEEDLE-WOMEN.................................. *Page* 76

CHAPTER X.
OLD LONDON 81

CHAPTER XI.
OUR HOUSES AND OUR HEALTH....................................... 88

CHAPTER XII.
EVILS IN CELLARS, SHOPS, AND YARDS 96

CHAPTER XIII.
TRAVELLERS BY SEA AND LAND 104

CHAPTER XIV..
GOOD COOKERY AND BAD COOKERY FOR THE MULTITUDE.................. 108

CHAPTER XV.
FRESH AIR IN THE COUNTRY 114

CHAPTER XVI.
WINDOW GARDENS, AND GARDEN SHOWS 124

LIST OF ILLUSTRATIONS.

FRONTISPIECE—A HOME IN BETHNAL GREEN.
HOUSE-TOPS FROM THE RAILWAY .... *Page* 2
PLEASANT PLACE, NEW SQUARE. PRETTY LODGINGS,—FOR PIGS 5
LIGHT AND AIR FOR THE CELLAR DWELLING 13
A BACK GARDEN IN NICHOL STREET, BETHNAL GREEN. 13
AN INFANT NURSERY: DAMP, UNDRAINED, AND ILL LIGHTED 20
AN EAST-END TEA-GARDEN, WITH SALUBRIOUS OUTSKIRTS 24
A DAMP ROOM; AND ITS DANGERS 27
A BEDROOM UNDER THE STAIRS 34
SLEEPING ACCOMMODATION FOR NINE CHILDREN 35
FAMILY STOWAGE; NINE SLEEPERS BESIDES DOG AND CAT 35
A MODERN HOUSE WITH THIRTY-FOUR OCCUPANTS 37
HEALTHFUL CONDITION OF A HOUSE IN ISLINGTON 39
A PESTILENT SUBURBAN COTTAGE 40
ARTIFICIAL FLOWER MAKERS; BLIGHTING THE BUDS 42
"WAKING" THE DEAD; AND KILLING THE LIVING 43
A VERY SICK ROOM 43
A SHOEMAKER'S WORKSHOP; MORE CARE FOR THE "SOLES" THAN THE BODIES.. 43
MURDERING THE INNOCENTS 44
THE CELLAR AND ITS PRODUCE 50
A PLEASANT LOOK-OUT 50
HOME COMFORT 51

LIST OF ILLUSTRATIONS.

A MEWS NEAR RUSSELL SQUARE	*Page* 53
WATER SUPPLY; NO SUPPLY. FRYINGPAN ALLEY, CLERKENWELL	54
SICKNESS IN THE WASHHOUSE, AND WHY	56
THE NORTH BANK OF THE THAMES: EAST OF BLACKFRIARS BRIDGE	58
ASHLIN'S PLACE, DRURY LANE. A LONDON DAIRY, 1863	64
A NARROW ALLEY IN THE COAL-YARD, DRURY LANE	68
BARLEY COURT. WHO SOWED THE TARES?	68
WYCH STREET, STRAND; AS SEEN LOOKING EAST	85
HOLYWELL STREET; ALSO LOOKING EAST	86
A BEER-CELLAR IN LONDON. "TAKING A DRAIN"	97
A CUT THROUGH A HOUSE IN THE CITY	99
A BERTH TO BRING DEATH	104
PACKING AND POISONING	106
COOKING AND WASTING	109
WASHING DAY	112
SWEETENING THE AIR OF THE COUNTRY: A VILLAGE IN ESSEX	116
POISONING THE SPRINGS: SITTINGBOURNE	119
PITMEN'S DWELLINGS IN THE NORTH. A REFINING PROSPECT	123
A WINDOW GARDEN	124

ANOTHER BLOW FOR LIFE.

CHAPTER I.

THE EAST OF LONDON.

Do you ever go East, good Reader? Something is to be learnt by doing so,—the miserable nature of the large mass of constructions around the metropolis, the wretched conditions under which many fellow-creatures dwell, and the undesirability of offering much obstruction to the proposed clearing away of such places by railway companies and others. Going thither from the West, do not overlook the sight to be obtained,—say between the hours of twelve and five,—from the guarded resting-place in the carriage-way from Cannon Street, Cheapside, and Fenchurch Street, to London Bridge. From the Docks come large covered vans, heavily laden with all descriptions of merchandise, the produce of every part of the world; while railway-vans, coal-wagons, the carts of the country carriers, carriages of the well-to-do, omnibuses, cabs, and other conveyances, form a struggling mass, seemingly inextricable. In all directions, far as the eye can reach, the footpaths too are thronged with countless wayfarers.

Hour after hour of the day, this vast tide of life continues to ebb and flow; and even in the night there is no stillness here. Noting this indescribable bustle, the incessant going and coming to and from the heart of the metropolis, and remembering that there are many other crowded thoroughfares, some notion may be obtained of the extent of the house accommodation required by the millions who cause this overflow. The scene which meets the eye shows the necessity of very speedy changes in the mode of transport of both goods and passengers. The rapid increase of the population, manufactures, and commerce of Great Britain is the world's wonder. Each week the difficulty at London Bridge will increase; and, without very speedy measures, a main artery closely connected with the heart of London will become congested, causing even greater loss and inconvenience than are now felt.

If an extra number of wagons travel from the Docks to the Borough, for a time the traffic is almost prevented. In slippery weather matters are worse; and if Cheapside roadway chance to need repair, the delay causes not only a considerable waste of time, but also loss of money. For these and other reasons it is most necessary to push forward the metropolitan railways as rapidly as possible. At present the various termini add to the overcrowding: when, however, the whole system has been fully carried out, the advantages will be evident. The road along the Thames, too, is no less essential.

It is not very easy to make way from the spot mentioned to Fenchurch Street station; but, that being done, you may, on the right hand and on the left, view from the railway the homes of people which are on the road to Stepney. We have sketched a morsel of the heap of rubbish (Fig. 1).

Fig. 1.—House-tops from the Railway.

Here are masses of houses, small in size, ill-constructed, without effective drainage, and in many other ways abominable. From the streets, bad as many of them are, stretch back-slums which are worse—slums in which human life is always in danger. Passing Mile End, we stop at Stepney; and wandering thence towards the Mile-End Road, it will be observed that in the Stepney district there are many wide streets and open squares. In some of the latter are houses and gardens which have once been pleasant, but have now fallen into decay. The neighbourhood would be healthy if it were supplied with pure water, and the drainage and paving in parts were improved; there is ample space for the buildings, and the soil is of that kind which gets rid of many impurities.

On the way to Mile-End Road, it may be observed that great improvements are going forward. Most of the houses of the silk-weavers in this locality—notwithstanding present unfortunate circumstances—have the neat appearance which we have in former books described as belonging to them. In several directions, the cottages—or, more properly speaking, hovels and huts—are giving way to more substantial buildings. At one point, a large space has been cleared, which it is hoped will be preserved open by the parish authorities. A large number of unwholesome houses, unfit for the occupation of families, have been cleared away; and wide roadways and paved footpaths are laid down, along which will be raised, it may be anticipated, substantial houses.

Objection has been made to the demolition of the residences of the working classes by men who are earnest in promoting the welfare of the industrious and poorer members of the community; and we have been amongst the foremost in calling for other provision for the occupants, where this is to take place. When, however, we consider the onward progress of this capital and the country generally—when it is seen that many of the new dwellings of the tradesmen and middle classes exhibit a marked improvement; and knowing too well that, in these districts the families of industrious workmen are placed in homes which weaken, degrade, and destroy them,—we cannot oppose the sweeping away of such charnel-houses. Inconvenience is felt during the time of transition, but good will result. Thousands who had been living in tenements that, during the last twenty or thirty years, have been pulled down, have found their way to houses which, although not what might be wished, are much better than those left; and in many localities we find even dustmen and costermongers in houses of a better character than they would formerly have ventured on.

From the gate turning westward there is a street in which there is a market for costermongers; the oily smell of frying fish, which is common in eastern parts, unpleasantly taints the air, and the scavengers do their duty very badly. Some of the little streets leading hence are planted with very small undrained houses; and from these run courts in which life must be a struggle. It will be to the advantage of those who now occupy these places if they are swept away. The closet accommodation is generally bad.

With difficulty we find our way to Barnsley Street, a place of evil repute, and one of the possessions of the miserly Mrs. Emsley, who supplied the poor with tenements which the people said were "not fit for dogs," and met with a terrible death. On the road are the church and schools of St. Bartholomew, Bethnal Green. We hear of streets in which every door would be thrown open for the shelter of a thief. We see in little bits of waste land groups of men and boys gambling. We hear terrible language, even from very young children. The bulk of the people, however, are decent hard-working persons; many of them earning very small wages, but remarkably intelligent, and anxious to get their children to school and themselves into better circumstances. There are indications of this in various quarters; for instance, in the maintenance of cheap schools and penny banks.

In this part of the metropolis, as in others, though the dwellings are dwarfed and dilapidated, the public-houses manage to keep up an appearance. They are gay with placards of "Unsophisticated Gin," "Reputation Ales," and "Jones's Gin at 4d. that speaks for itself," or makes others do so in a way not very desirable. The houses in Barnsley Street have been improved, but close by are many dwellings in a most neglected condition; for instance, in Pleasant Street. Behind it was a square of most wretched and dilapidated houses, as our sketch shows (Fig. 2). In the centre some people had planted caravans, in which their families lived. The Square has been improved, but the street remains in a wretched state; and there are worse branches from this spot — slums occupied with every kind of filth and refuse. It is not for such places as these — places disgraceful to this great city, and unfit for the occupation of man—that we should strive to stay the progress of improvement.

Fig. 2.—" Pleasant Place," New Square. Pretty Lodgings—for Pigs.

The condition of the weavers of Spitalfields is constantly growing more hopeless.

Always bearing with patience suffering and distress—always anxious for employment,—the weavers have gone on from bad to worse, until they now seem to have fallen into despair, and means are being taken to enable a certain number of them to emigrate or remove to some better field for labour. Years ago we directed attention to the Spitalfields silk trade, and recommended the course which is now suggested. The result of the struggle between hand and steam looms was certain. Notwithstanding the shrewdness of the majority of the weavers in political and other questions, it was not easy to get them to understand the principles which govern the price of labour. They have from time to time petitioned Parliament for the imposition of high rates of duty on foreign silks imported, but they were not anxious to improve their skill in design; and, notwithstanding the great modern improvements in machinery, they continued using the same kind of looms as their fathers and grandfathers had done. They worked singly or in families, without any general organization; and the pressure of the times, and other circumstances, left them in a measure at the mercy of capitalists. Although the evils which threatened Spitalfields were seen by many others, the weavers were unwilling to believe in the distress that was coming upon them, and were at times angry with those who, taking broad and general views, endeavoured to lead them for their own good. Nor can we much wonder at this, when we consider that several generations have been reared to this kind of work; the families of the weavers, originally of a foreign stock, have married one with another, and they are generally, in a most remarkable degree, attached to their homes and gardens. The looms used by the men and women are property in which they take interest, and the general disposition of the workers inclined them to hope for beneficial changes, though these in the ordinary course of affairs were not likely to occur.

As a contrast to the condition in which the Spitalfields weavers are placed —large families by their united exertions unable to procure the necessaries of life; young girls and boys, by the aid of the old-fashioned machine, unable to earn more than a few pence in the week by the labour of silk-winding,— we look abroad, into various parts of England, and find that, with but few exceptions, the remuneration of the labouring classes of the country has been steadily progressing, and that both food and clothing have been considerably lowered in price. Macaulay has shown that, towards the close of the seventeenth century, all classes were paid less wages than they are now. Agricultural labourers received only from 2s. to 3s. a week with food, or from 4s. to 5s. without. In 1661, the justices at Chelmsford fixed the rate at 6s. in winter and 7s. in summer: at this time all the necessaries of life were dear. In 1730, the daily earnings of bricklayers and mechanics employed at Greenwich Hospital averaged 2s. 6d. a day, with bread dearer than at present. Even in 1800, the wages of a good mason in London were only 16s. a week, when wheat was 90s. 6d. a quarter. The same class of workmen are now receiving 33s. a week, and all kinds of clothing material, silk included, are greatly reduced in cost since 1800.

It is to be hoped that means will be forthcoming to try the experiment on a large scale of enabling families from Spitalfields to remove to places where their labour may be directed into other channels profitable to themselves and useful to others. It is, unfortunately, the case, that, even in need, it is difficult to prevail on English workmen to change their pursuits. We have noticed hundreds of persons who have waited to be reduced to beggary by changes in certain branches of trade, rather than turn their hands to some other kind of work which they were well able to manage.

The Bethnal Green "Union," which is a spacious building, is full, and contains but a small proportion of the number who receive parish relief in this poor and now distressed district. We fear, too, that for some time, if measures are not used to avert it, the extent of pauperism will be greatly increasing. There are various causes for this. The introduction of the sewing-machine is affecting the local tailors, needlewomen, and those engaged in the manufacture of boots, shoes, and many other articles. Steam-machinery and other introductions have made profitless various branches of industry. We live, indeed, in an age of wonderful change; and while measures are in progress for the general good, a large amount of suffering and distress falls on particular classes. Such being the case, we require new means for assisting those who are particularly affected by the present state of transition.

Inquiry induces a feeling of admiration for the patience and worth of the chief part of the people. Going from house to house we hear the same tale told, and see half-famished and ill-clad children. We notice that, in nine cases out of ten, there is no chance for their future welfare, unless means are used which do not at the present time exist. At the corners of the streets may be seen groups of youths of the age of from sixteen to twenty (evidently not of the vicious class), lean, wan, and ragged. On speaking to these lads, they will tell you that they are the sons of silk-weavers: they have no employment: some have tried to get into a man-of-war, but being over fifteen years of age, have been refused: they have tried to enlist into the army, but their chest or height would not pass inspection. *What is to become of such as these?* Many of them would do well in the colonies: good air, sufficient food, and employment, would soon improve their condition, and make them useful in those lands where labour is wanted, and the earth is fertile.

The public has heard lately that some poor creatures have died of actual starvation. In the houses we find young women who have no employment, and who might, under proper care and guidance, be useful in the colonies, or they might be employed as domestic servants, or in some other way, at home.

To confirm what we have said, we will note the particulars of a few cases which, in the course of a walk, came under our notice. The first was that of a young couple. The wife had been a domestic servant before marriage. The business of the husband was that of brush-drawing, by which he had been enabled to earn 18s. a week. Work had become dull, and for some time he had been without his usual employment, and had sought some other as a labourer at the docks. During the last fortnight he had had three days' work at 2s. 6d. a day (7s. 6d.). The rent of the room occupied by these people was 2s. 3d. a week. At times, but not as it appears driven to it by actual want, the wife had obtained work at a pickling warehouse, and could earn from 9d. to 1s. a day. Now through ill-health she is unable to attend to this duty, and is obliged to apply to the parish for medical assistance. This is a bad beginning. We then found a man forty-six years of age, who had been formerly a plumber and glazier, but being unable, in consequence of lameness, to follow that employment, he now works at winding the cotton used for making fringe. In the course of a week, if the material were favourable, he could earn from 3s. to 3s. 6d.; at some times not more than 2s. 6d. The wife found occasional employment in washing: the whole income was not more on the average than 7s. 6d. a week; and there were, besides the man and his wife, two children to support. Our next visit was to the home of a silk-weaver, who occupies the top part of a house, every part of which is crowded with people. With difficulty we ascended the dark, narrow, and ill-constructed staircase. There were several hand-looms—all empty, except one, at which the daughter was at work, who, by long and hard labour, could earn 5s. a week — a sum but little more than sufficient to pay the rent. The man and his wife had lived on the same spot for many years. "Forty years ago," said the weaver, "I could readily earn

£2. 10s. a week; now I could not earn more than from 9s. to 10s., and work is not easily to be had. If a little present assistance be given, things will work round; times will mend—anything rather than go into the union." In several other instances, we noticed the same hopeful feeling: these people, seemingly, forget the regular decline of prices, and that now, when they have fallen so low that they are not sufficient for support, work is still not easily to be found. With the exception of the looms there was no furniture of any worth. In such a case as this, the young daughters might emigrate with great advantage to themselves; but they would not like to leave their father and mother, who are getting old. And so they stop,—and starve.

In the house of one weaver the children were ill with small-pox; one of them lying in a small, close, and stifling room. There the man was without employment, and had been nearly so since last Christmas. Before then for some time his work, and the help of some of the children at silk-winding, had not produced more, after the rent was paid, than from 6s. to 7s. a week. Intelligent in many respects, it is a matter for regret that ignorance of social and sanitary laws generally prevails: these might with but little trouble be readily taught. When a silk-weaver will gravely tell you that the present state of business is caused by "Gladstone,"—not mentioning that gentleman's name with particular favour,—if we lay our hand upon his old-fashioned loom and say, "It would be just as possible for the old stage-wagon to compete with the locomotive as for you to contend with steam-power silk-looms;" he can only add, "Well, at any rate, it is very hard for us." When reminded of the present price of bread and other necessaries of life in comparison with the uncertainty in this respect of other times, he comprehends the matter readily. Great good might be done not only amongst the silk-weavers, but also amongst those who are connected with other depressed branches of industry by the spread of sound information.

The sanitary state of the district is miserably bad. Notwithstanding all that has been said on the subject, the horrible condition in which a vast population are living is not understood and realized by the public. Nothing short of a personal examination, indeed, under proper guidance, can convey a complete idea of it. We will endeavour, however, by bringing the pencil to the aid of the pen, to make the facts a little clearer, and to urge on the authorities the absolute necessity for immediate steps with a view to bringing about a better state of things. Some of these steps, moreover, are quite practicable and not difficult. The Bethnal Green Vestry has met, and the Guardians have met, and have endeavoured to cast discredit upon Dr. Moore, one of their medical officers, who gave evidence on recent inquests proving the evil state of the place, and to show that the condition of the parish is of the most creditable and satisfactory description. They accuse Dr. Moore of past doings, which, if correctly described, should have forced them before now to dismiss that gentleman from his office,—an office of vast importance to the poor. They quibble on the meaning of "blood-poisoning," and, in spite of the startling revelations which have been made from time to time for many years past, the Board profess to be blind to the evils with which they are surrounded. Ultimately, they pass a resolution, calling on the Poor-Law Commissioners to sanction Dr. Moore's dismissal from his office of Medical Officer of part of this district. Nine members of the Board voted for the dismissal, three against it, and four declined to vote either way. We do not regret this result, inasmuch as it affords hope of a searching inquiry that may be the means of obliging the Board of Guardians to do their duty.

We should like to know how many of the majority of nine are interested in the poisonous and dilapidated dwellings in the parish. The Government, through the Privy Council, should order an independent, extensive, and careful investigation to be made by persons whom they might appoint. They should hear from Inspector Price what number of cellars are occupied in a condition contrary to the law, and to the great damage of life and health. The Building Act should be brought to bear upon the dangerous and dilapidated dwellings which exist. Blocks of houses should be examined, and a note taken of the population of each room. The extent and nature of the water supply should be learnt; also, the nature of the closet accommodation, and the manner in which the dust-contractors and street scavengers do, or rather do not do, their duty. If this inquiry were rightly carried out, we should see where the blame really rests.

As matters stand at present, the official arrangements for the preservation of the public health are wholly insufficient. There is only one sanitary inspector for this large district, which requires three or four active and intelligent men; and each day shows that the solitary inspector is unfit for his work.

We have recently again carefully examined a considerable part of the district, including Grey-Eagle Street and the courts at the back of it, Phœnix Street, Nichol Street and its courts, Old Nichol Street, Half Nichol Street, and other places. With few exceptions, each room contains a separate family; some consisting of mother, father, and eight children. The first two adjoining houses that we looked into, of six rooms each, contained forty-eight persons. To supply these with water, a stream runs for ten or twelve minutes each day, except Sunday, from a small tap at the back of one of the houses. The struggle for it is sometimes great: the means of storage are very small. The result is, that on Sunday (as we have pointed out in previous publications) there is seldom a drop of water to be had, and this of itself leads to a whole train of evils. The houses are, of course, ill-ventilated. The front room in the basement, wholly below the ground, dark and damp, is occupied, at a cost of 2s. a week for rent. We tried our old test on the first two women seen standing at the doors. "How many children have you?" "Four," was the reply of the first of them. "Have you lost any?" "Five, and there is one inside given over by the doctor." The second had two living, and had lost three. Many of the houses are in a dangerous state structurally, and some have been condemned under the Building Act. Here is the description the inspector of nuisances gave of these when he went to the magistrate at Worship Street on the subject. He said each room contained a man and his wife and six or seven children. The whole were filthy and dilapidated; the party-wall between Nos. 20 and 21 bulged at the basement to the extent of at least two feet, and the whole brickwork throughout was so much fractured that it might fall at any moment. In the basement of No. 20, a great quantity of the dust and house-refuse had not been removed for fourteen years, and formed a mound, through which a pathway had been made, by constant treading, which led from and to the entrances at the back and front. The water for drinking purposes was derived from a small tub without a lid in the midst of this heap; but a very scanty supply was furnished, it not being "on" much more than twenty minutes at a time. There was no efficient drainage to take off the waste water, so that the basements were saturated by it, and pools of stagnant water collected in the yards, which were unpaved, and contained a quantity of putrid vegetables, that had been in that position for a long time!

In George Street, three children have died in one house, and the rest of the family have been made ill, through the want of pure air!

The occupation of underground rooms here, as well as elsewhere, is illegal, and may at once be prevented. Under the Local Management Act, an underground room may not be occupied separately as a dwelling unless certain conditions are complied with, one of which is that there shall be a window of specified size, with an area before it open down to six inches below the floor of the room. The terms of the Act, however, have led to the belief that the duty of discovering the occupancy of such rooms rests with the district surveyor appointed under the Building Act, whose duties are entirely structural, who is quite unfit to serve as sanitary policeman, and, moreover, has not power under the Act to prove his case if he were to try. For the most part, therefore, the Act is nugatory,—we had nearly written, with Hood, *Newgatory*,— excepting where, as in Islington and some other parishes, the inspector of nuisances, or other qualified person, obtains the proof of occupancy, calls on the district surveyor for a report as to the structural deficiency only, and carries the case before a magistrate in accordance with the Act. This should at once be done in Bethnal Green, and scores of murderous dens would be shut up. It is no answer to say the inhabitants prefer to live, or (more truly) to die, in such rooms rather than meet the difficulty of finding a better room elsewhere. They must not be allowed to do so. Suicide is not permitted; still less, suicide that leads to the death of others not desiring to die, and to the pauperizing of a still larger number, who must be maintained by the more sensible and provident.

One of the worst examples that we saw of these underground rooms we must endeavour to illustrate. It is in Nichol Street, No. 59, and may be described as entirely below the surface. The window of the apartment is a little over three feet in width, and about the same in height: the area is even with the breadth and depth of the window. It extends from the wall about two feet, and was originally closed with an iron grating; but this having become broken, the entire top of the area has been covered with wood, so that the only means of light and ventilation is a chink three feet wide by four and a half inches in height (Fig. 3). Passing through the passage to the back, the dilapidated condition of the premises, as may be seen in the sketch, is startling (Fig. 4). The plaster within has fallen from the walls and ceilings, the narrow staircase is rotten and shaky, the general colour is of a dingy smoky black, with peeps of indifferent brickwork and broken laths. At the back there is a large open space, in a most filthy condition; damp refuse of all kinds is piled up against the wall; there is no supply of water; the people have "to hunt for it;" nor is there any distinct closet accommodation for this house.

Fig. 3.—Light and Air for the Cellar Dwelling.

When looking at the wet and poisonous mound, at the ill-built wall through which the damp and unwholesome matter

Fig. 4.—A Back Garden in Nichol Street, Bethnal Green.

must weep, and seeing in all directions similar neglect of proper scavenging, we cannot but insist that this state of things is disgraceful to the parish.

But as regards the cellar, in all our experience of London destitution and awful conditions, we have seen nothing more harrowing than what there met the view.* Through the narrow space of the window that is left open there came a glimmering light, which fell upon two figures on a broken truckle, seemingly naked, with the exception of some black rags passed across the middle of the bodies; but the greater part of the room, small as it is, was in total darkness. In this profound depth our sagacious guide, Mr. Price, thought that there were more figures visible; and on asking if any were there, a female voice replied, "Yes; here are two of us. Mother is out." And gradually, as the eye became accustomed to the gloom, two other figures were to be seen lying in a corner upon rags. This was between twelve and one o'clock in the day. We were not disposed to look further into their mystery; but it was evident that one of the unfortunates was resting close to the damp and poisonous wall. Neither words nor drawing can convey a complete idea of this den and its thick and polluted atmosphere. Instead of being filled with the pure life-giving air which is needful for human existence, it seemed occupied by something which might be moved and weighed. The height of the room, all of which is below the surface, is not quite six feet. The window would not open; the ceiling was ready to fall; and the walls, so far as the light showed, were damp and mildewed. The lodgers here were a widow and her four children; one a girl twenty years of age, another girl eighteen, a boy of fourteen, and a boy of twelve. What, we ask, is to become of those unhappy creatures, reared in the dark and the dirt, and of the multitude who in this metropolis are "dragged up" under similar circumstances?

For four such rooms as we have attempted to describe there are paid on the whole 12s. a week; that is, £31. 4s. per year. Another similar cellar, not quite so dark or so damp, we found occupied by a man and his wife and six children, aged respectively fourteen, eleven, nine, six, and four years, and one ten months. We could draw a frightful picture of what met our sight in an upper room of a neighbouring house, but it would not further our present object, which is practical and precise,—to call for a sufficient water supply; the periodical removal, at short intervals, of all refuse; and the enforcement of the law in respect of the occupancy of underground dwellings.

We returned from the inspection saddened and ill. We have written of it coolly, but it was a sight to move indignation.

* See Frontispiece.

BLOOD-POISONING.

Through the startling events that have occurred in this neighbourhood there is great excitement in connection with blood poisoning,—as it is now popularly called,—in Bethnal Green: the Government and even the parish authorities have been roused to make a show of exertion; so that many feel a hope that now something effectual will be done to put an end to existing disgrace and danger. We trust that these anticipations may prove correct; but many disappointments in this way have rendered us doubtful, and lead us still to fear that when the Press, thinking sufficient has been written to effect a beneficial change, have relaxed in their vigilance, things will be allowed to relapse into their former state. The parish authorities look carelessly at the sickness and death around them, and sceptically and contemptuously at the actual causes, discouraging the medical officers when they bring to their notice too true reports of the shocking state of suffering which exists. The absolute necessity for important changes in the management of many thousands of the metropolitan dwellings is so evident, that the need of them must eventually be perceived by the Legislature. Within five weeks, five children of one family have all perished from exactly the same disorder as that attributed on a previous inquiry, viz., a "poisoning of the blood," through the impurity of the air, the bad water supply, and other defective sanitary conditions.

At one inquest it was stated that in the twenty-two houses forming Thorold Square, twenty children had been attacked with illness, and that twelve of these had died. The Roger family occupied one room, and were ten in number,—eight children and the father and mother. Here, even without any other cause, the overcrowding was sufficient to produce pestilence: but George Stratford, a weaver, tells us that there had been no water supplied to any of the houses but three for eighteen months, except through a broken and unuseable pump. In the heat of the summer they never had a pailful of water at any time for three weeks, except what they begged from others as best they could. The closets had no pans, and were not trapped: in fact, they might be called cesspools: sometimes they were empty, but he had seen them running over with soil. There were sixty families in the square, and about 350 children among them.

Even the wholesale slaughter here is not to be wondered at when we find people oppressed by every sanitary neglect; living in rooms dirty and without ventilation, to the number of nine or ten in each—and frequently with more at night.

The insanitary state of neighbourhoods that, month after month, and year after year, remain unmitigated in their filth, unless some fever or other pestilence break out, might, even in the present state of the law, be greatly improved; and such a state of things as exists only too evidently shows that, in East London, the parish inspectors, as they at present exercise their functions, are next to useless.

It is imperative that houses let to various lodgers should be systematically and carefully inspected, and made sanitarily habitable. There should be no possibility of twenty-two houses swarming with people being left for weeks without water, with choked closets and imperfect drains. To effect what is needed must not be left to parish authorities, but be placed in the hands of a power quite independent, and not likely to be biassed by either local or personal considerations. Throughout the metropolitan district all the dwelling-houses which are sub-let into more than a certain number of tenements should be placed, with certain restrictions, under the inspection of properly qualified persons, who should be empowered to grant *licences for the letting* of these places, provided that their condition were satisfactory. A measure of this kind, well managed, would, to a considerable extent, remove one of the foulest blots of the metropolis. There are many houses, now pest-places, which, with proper sanitary care, might be made fit for human habitation; and, along with this improvement, would come a beneficial alteration in the health, state, and manners of the people.

CHAPTER II.

INFANTICIDE WITHOUT INTENTION.

MURDER has been classed amongst the *fine* arts, *coarse* as a good deal of it no doubt is in practice. There are many ways of getting rid of *surplus* infants. It is not merely by cutting the throats of the poor little innocents as if they were pigs, or by drowning them as if they were kittens, that thousands of murders are effected. In China they go about it in a more matter-of-fact and business-like way than we do; but throwing them in heaps, alive, within the precincts of a "devil's temple," there to perish, does not come up to our more refined and civilized and varied modes of doing the Malthusianly needful work. And, in speaking of refined and civilized operations of the sort, it is not simply meant to refer to reiterated doses of "quietness" and such-like drugs; nor even to ingenious processes such as those of the talented individual who got rid of five of his superfluous progeny by various artful dodges; such as setting a tub of water, like a trap, for the unprotected little one to roll into out of bed, when all were asleep, and when no one, therefore, was to blame. Perhaps the method most entitling infanticide to be regarded as a branch (we wish we could call it a dead branch) of the fine arts, is to choke them by degrees, from short supplies of vital air, in close apartments. This is a much more safe and artful way of "keeping down the population" than either smothering them in bed, dosing them with laudanum, or even stuffing them with "strong meat" in the place of milk.

The newspapers make a tremendous outcry when some poor "unfortunate" young woman has been driven, by the force of public indignation, to cast her little one into a pond or a river; especially if the outcast excite general indignation still farther by failing at the same time to commit self-murder; but how serenely the public contemplate that wholesale infanticide which disposes of 40 or 45 children out of *every* 100 before they are five years old! There are some who wink at such a state of matters; arguing that "it is a providential mercy so many die; because, if all the children of the poor lived, the poor-rates required for their maintenance would be increased by two-fifths, and even more;" but, unfortunately for the force of this Malthusian argument, wholesale death implies wholesale sickness and want of stamina in infancy on the part of those who live; and foundations so weak are reared into frames so shaky that poor-law burdens must be immensely augmented, rather than diminished, by a high rate of infant mortality. Moreover, in a limited island-space such as that of Great Britain, the true greatness of the nation and its ability to sustain its poor could not but be vastly increased, were the foundations of life well and securely laid by improved arrangements promotive of health and vigour, so as to raise the stamina of its manhood to a high pitch. And it is not the improved *physique* of the matured man alone that would thus be realized: the fact that vigorous parents lead to a vigorous progeny is no less obvious; and thus the nation would improve, physically speaking, in an accelerated ratio, were more care and attention given to the rearing of infants.

On the Bridge of Life—described in that beautiful physiological allegory, "The Vision of Mirza,"—are shown, in the early stages of the passage, many rents and pitfalls through which multitudes of passengers drop, to rapidly disappear in the waters beneath, which flow darkly along. Towards the middle the danger is lessened, and a powerful and compact band move steadily onwards, with comparatively small loss, until the middle of the bridge is gained, when the dangerous pitfalls increase again in number, so that only two or three solitary pilgrims are left at the further end, who also ultimately disappear. Such is the general rule of life: the weak and tender infant is subject to injury from the slightest causes: it can be easily suffocated, as by bed-clothes, or even while in the nurse's arms. Its life is extinguished by unwholesome air, and by those numerous neglects which are common. But admitting—as we are not inclined to admit—that, in passing the first arches of the bridge of life, there must naturally and necessarily be more deaths than towards the second and middle stages of the journey; still, there can be no doubt that by preventable causes, in the present conditions of society in this country, more than twice as many deaths then happen as would, with proper arrangements, occur.

The Privy Council, impressed with this fact and the need of amendment, appointed medical men to make inquiry into this most important subject; and Dr. Greenhow, one of the staff, remarks that in the manufacturing districts he frequently found, on questioning married factory-women, that two-thirds or three-fourths of the children born to them had died in infancy. They are deprived of the warmth of their mothers' bosom; left to the care of strangers; fed on unsuitable food; and, when they dwindle and become fractious, are drugged with opiates; for those who have to work in the day cannot do so if they are disturbed at night. One druggist alone, a member of the Nottingham Town Council, states that he sells about 400 gallons of laudanum annually, at least one-half of which he believes to be administered to infants. Dr. Greenhow notices the grievous extent to which parents, who intrust the management of children largely to strangers, get demoralized towards their offspring; becoming more or less indifferent about them. As so many children die, the mothers become familiarized with the fact, and speak of the death of their children with a degree of nonchalance rarely met with amongst women who devote themselves mainly to the care of their offspring.

Mr. Simon, in presenting his report to the Privy Council, observes that such a picture of suffering and demoralization is very sad. The poor factory-woman, who meant only to sell her honest industry, gradually finds that she has sold everything which other women understand as happiness. The law cannot reach the evil; but he suggests, with reference to one part of it, that masters might establish within their own factories, under well-advised regulations, nursery-rooms, where working mothers might leave their infants in some proper and kindly charge, and might, as often as necessary, have access to them. This is a good suggestion, and would prove of decided advantage, if it could be carried out. We know the evil conditions of infant nurseries in the manufacturing districts, where female labour is largely in demand. In many instances the infants are left for hours in the charge of other children not much bigger than themselves, or are locked up during the long absence of the mother. There is a kind of nursery, however, presided over by imbecile and often cross old women, who, in their own youth, had never been accustomed to the proper care of children: these guardians often inhabit unventilated and unwholesome rooms in undrained houses; and from morning till night, in too many instances, as well as from night till morning, the little creatures are stupified by the administration of "quietness," as the women call the laudanum and other narcotic mixtures administered to children who are fretful.

Here is a sketch of one of these nurseries, outside and in (Fig. 5),—A showing the entrance-door and the only window. It is not far from Manchester; half underground, and wholly damp and unfit. The majority of the children had been "quieted," when we called. We all know, in respect of potatoes, what sort of growth takes place in a cellar.

From these dismal pictures let us turn to more pleasant prospects;—to large well-ventilated rooms, arranged with the greatest neatness; an even temperature winter and summer; snug little beds ranged around, with sheets of snowy whiteness; a play-place of soft felt or carpet, with toys, in the centre; intelligent attendants; baths; wholesome food, and other accommodations; while the charge made to mothers for all this is small, not exceeding, if we take one thing

Fig. 5.—An Infant Nursery: Damp, Undrained, and Ill-lighted.

with another, the cost of the mismanagement of the old women. And yet, strange to say, the latter and their dingy dens are better liked, by a great majority of the persons to whom good infant nurseries would prove beneficial, than places which are patterns of order, and provided with all that is essential to health.

A certain number of poor persons, who have more than the usual share of the intelligence of their class, have sent their children to the infant nurseries which have been opened in some parts of the metropolis and in other large towns; but this institution has not as yet spread to the extent to which it was hoped that it would. Means should be used to diffuse a knowledge of the laws of health, and to show to the workers who are verging on womanhood the advantages that would result from placing their infants under proper care; without the chance of the administration of laudanum and other poisons of a similar nature; and where they would not be injured by the foul, close air of the rooms in which too often delicate infants are kept in dirt and neglect.

Homes for pauper children are advocated by a member of the Ladies' Sanitary Association, in a tract issued by that association,* and which merits circulation. It is proposed that these homes should consist simply of improved arrangements, at the cost and under the authority of the poor-law guardians, carried out in each parish or union. Such homes, it is suggested, would also serve as schools, in which nurses, pupil-teachers, school-mistresses, governesses, adult girls, and young mothers of any class could learn the best mode of practically managing infants and little children, so far as regards their physical well-being. There might thus be obtained fees to increase the funds applicable to such homes; which, moreover, would not, it is believed, cost more than pauper infants and children cost the guardians and the rate-payers under the present *system*—if we can so call it.

The subject of Children's Hospitals is one on which a few words should be said.

It is a frightful circumstance that the mortality of children under ten years of age is only 2 per cent. less than it was fifty years ago;—so that, of 50,000 persons, for example, dying annually in London, 21,000 are children under that age. Notwithstanding the immense extent of sickness which must have preceded this multitude of deaths, there is no adequate accommodation in the London hospitals for sick children. In consequence of the great need of such

* Office, No. 14A, Princes Street, Cavendish Square, London, W.

an establishment, some earnest persons, by great exertions, succeeded in opening an hospital for children in Great Ormond Street, where many receive advice and medicine. This should be aided.

Returning to our starting-point, we would again and again re-urge, that if we would have sound men and women, who make a sound people, we must look after the babies. The present wholesale murder without intention, which is allowed to go on, is a disgrace to our civilization.

CHAPTER III.

HIDDEN DANGERS—AN EAST-END TEA-GARDEN.

THE risks that people run every day, without knowing of their existence, are often much greater than those which give them the greatest uneasiness. They are frightened by a squib that cannot hurt them, and sit contentedly week after week on a barrel of gunpowder with a lighted fuse within an inch of the bung-hole, not believing in the danger till they find themselves blown into the air.

Some years ago, when looking to the state of the banks of the Thames near the outlet of the Fleet-ditch, we met with an artist whose business kept him employed in the City, walking along the dirty margin; and on asking what could have led him to such a locality, we were answered that he had "just stepped out to get a breath of fresh air!" You may see other artists among the willows overhanging death-distilling water-pools, or busily sketching the luxuriant herbage on the banks of stagnant brooks or ditches. Pent-up Londoners seek recreation in most unwholesome places, without reason or consideration of the risk they run. Children not long ago were taken regularly to be aired in the reeking graveyards of the metropolis; and people of rank and fashion overcrowd certain ill-ventilated theatres and concert-rooms. Old-fashioned tradesmen still visit nightly for recreation the coffee-rooms and parlours of antiquated "publics," where, while discussing politics and parish affairs, the atmosphere, through the want of ventilation and space, is little short of poisonous.

Some rush to Boulogne, for the sake of their health! others to sea-side towns and fishing villages, where ventilation or drainage has not been thought of, and where the shore is strewn with putrefying fish and other refuse. Without, however, going further just now, let us glance at one of the suburban "tea-gardens," where, on Sundays and holidays, Londoners, with their wives and families, may be seen evidently taking a great deal of enjoyment and very moderate refreshment. On the roofs of taverns where a view can be had over green trees and fields, large numbers assemble to enjoy the air. From Bagnigge-wells the tea-gardens of the north of London have marched to Islington, Camden-town, and Kentish-town; thence to Hampstead, Hornsey, and elsewhere; and they are springing up in more distant parts. Rosherville and many other places are now made almost as convenient by railway as Hampstead and Highgate formerly were. In these tea-gardens the cabined Londoners and their children take their pleasure in bowers and arbours: they walk in shady places, and amongst beds of flowers; in some instances minstrelsy and singing enlivening the scene. We will not severely criticise the artistic taste displayed in the decoration of some of these places, but would consider how well or ill they are adapted for the promotion of health. Some are properly situated, and removed from offensive matter; but in others, sanitary care has been so much neglected that health must suffer rather than be improved by a visit. Look at our picture of an actual Eastend Tea-garden (Fig. 6): view the black stagnant ditch, which, hidden by

Fig. 6.—An East-end Tea garden, with Salubrious Outskirts.

trees from the view of the pleasure-seekers, girdles the bowers, arbours, and grounds, and stretches away like a huge black serpent towards newly-erected buildings. Avoid such tea-gardens, and the proprietors will find it to their benefit to provide healthful arrangements, and perhaps advertise not only the picturesque beauty and other attractions of their domain, but that "every care has been taken to make the sanitary conditions of the grounds complete, drainage having been carefully attended to, and all offensive matter removed from the neighbourhood."

It is very difficult, in examining a dwelling, to learn, without disturbing the premises, whether there are cesspools or not; for, in many instances, the disguise of the pits of pestilence is so artfully managed that it is only by the actual removal of parts of the closet that the truth can be ascertained. The results of these disguised cesspools are in many cases frightful. Some time ago the cesspool of a house, of which we knew, was disguised; and it is worth while to record the circumstances connected with it.—The cesspool* had been covered over and trapped: of course, it was speedily filled with liquid, which became daily more impure: this was passed to the imperfect drain, and to the untrapped sinks. Moreover, the whole basement of the house was impregnated with impure matter. The upper part of the house (three rooms) was occupied by a family of eight persons (six children—the wife was soon after arrival confined). At the time of removal to this place, a more healthy-looking group of children could not be seen: but soon after, arriving from a place where the drainage was complete, the complexion of the children became daily more pallid. It was difficult, notwithstanding all endeavours, to get ventilation at night, and to rise in the morning, in consequence of a heavy drowsiness. In a few weeks the children were more or less troubled with eruptions of the skin. Soon after four of them were attacked by measles—in two instances followed by hooping-cough, and in another by low fever. After the confinement of the wife she became in great danger. The infant from its birth had a cough that seriously affected its chest. The eldest child failed in health, and was, eventually, seized with rheumatic fever. It should be mentioned, that this ill-conditioned habitation was situated in rather a low position, not far from the Regent's Canal: this, no doubt, added to the evil. Besides the ill-health mentioned, a young man, living in the lower part of the premises, had a very serious attack of typhus fever, about the time that the infant and another child were suffering from bronchitis, which soon ended fatally in

* The closets of three houses drained into it.

the case of the former. We will not maintain that something of this might not have happened under other circumstances; but since the removal of the family to a healthy locality, the improvement in their condition is as remarkable as its change for worse was on the other occasion.

An example like this may have more weight than a volume of precepts.

Knowing the damage which is often done to buildings by damp, and the serious danger to health which arises from this cause, it is extraordinary to find, in many instances, how little care is taken effectually to drain the ground surrounding dwellings, and otherwise to keep them dry.

In the metropolitan suburbs, and in many places both in town and country, there is especial reason for complaint in this respect. Pools of stagnant water are allowed to collect and remain during the winter months. The land becomes saturated with moisture, which is more or less absorbed by the porous brick walls of the houses; and still further mischief is done by the summer heat distributing the evil contents in vapour throughout the surrounding locality. No care is taken in putting in the foundations.

The injurious effects and great extent of the evil in cottages and other dwellings are generally not sufficiently considered. In hundreds of instances, notwithstanding that large fires are regularly kept burning, the interior of rooms, even in houses occupied by persons of means and intelligence, is as moist as that of some caves: the paper peels off the walls; the plaster cracks and falls to pieces; the covers of books become mouldy, and have a musty smell; papers stored in cupboards, prints hanging against the walls, linen in drawers, if not constantly aired, soon perish. In mild, dull weather, streams of water run down the glass of the windows; and in frosty weather the glass is covered with icy crystals. At times the paint-work seems in a state of violent perspiration. In such houses, ironwork, both polished and of other kinds, gets rusty in a few hours. But these and other evils are as nothing in comparison with the ill effect produced upon health. The cause of the illness, however, is usually looked for in another direction. In many cases, the mischief is caused by want of attention to the spouts and pipes, which get stopped or broken; and in rainy weather streams of water fall upon the outer walls and sink into the basement; for in many small dwellings sufficient attention has not been paid, as we have said, to the foundations, and to the means of carrying away the

EVILS OF DAMP.   27

rain-water. Even if the spouts are in good condition, such is the nature of the building materials, and neglect of drainage, that the dampness from the earth may be seen to rise to one row of bricks after another;—to a height of from ten to twelve feet and upwards; and it is in such situations that many diseases, particularly among young children, are fostered if not generated.

In parts of the City and closely-populated portions of the metropolitan districts, much mischief is caused by the overflow of cisterns: the ball-cock is taken off, or pipes are allowed to become stopped or broken; and neighbours are surprised to find dampness appearing through walls in the most inconvenient situations. As regards damp houses, it is not always easy for inexperienced persons to detect them, particularly in the summer time. In order to catch a tenant, the exterior is smartly done up; the little plot of flowers and plants

Fig. 7.—A Damp Room; and its Dangers.

looks pleasant; and in the inside every room is decked with the "sweetest" papering. In a short time, however, a change takes place; and, in spite of care, the colours and patterns fade, and give the appearance of half a century's neglect.

The apartment which is shown in the engraving (Fig. 7) was carefully drawn on the spot. It is a room on the first floor of a house not far from the last one spoken of. Not nine months ago the wall-papering was renewed, and now it has almost perished, in one part, from the overflow of the spouts; ghastly forms have appeared in other parts; and from the ground the damp has risen up in the way we have endeavoured to illustrate.

Too much care cannot be taken to prevent the action of damp; and any necessary sum expended for this purpose will in the end be a saving. Damage is often done by the damp site on which buildings are placed; and yet, at the present time, we could point to new streets where the scavengers are depositing liquid sweepings, masses of decomposing animal and vegetable refuse, and other abominations; and upon these, presently, the walls of houses will be raised, without the slightest arrangement to keep down the moisture, or prevent dangerous exhalations. Those who sleep in the basement of a house so placed suffer first and most.

CHAPTER IV.

THE DANGERS OF OVERCROWDING.

LONG ago, in previous publications, we pointed out the evils that followed the removal of masses of houses in the metropolis, occupied by the poorer classes, without the provision of other dwellings in the neighbourhood of their means of living. We have seen with our own eyes, after such a clearing, the occupants of a single room increased from one family to three, from three families to *five*. We have seen this in Whitechapel, in Marylebone, and in Clerkenwell. When 1,500 people were ejected from Orchard Place, Portman Square, about nine years ago, we followed some of them, step by step, and saw that the eviction resulted in a dangerous addition to already thickly-crowded parts of the metropolis.* "Destroy the nest, and the rooks will fly away," said a Scotch Reformer, speaking of drones of the Church. And so say some now who deplore the condition of other "rookeries," and would give the occupants a larger area and better conditions. We have asked that some enactment should be made to lead railway companies and others to provide accommodation, to some extent at any rate, for those who are displaced. Lord Derby, when he recently made a step towards this in the House of Peers, pointed out that while the population of the City parishes had remained stationary, the number of houses since 1801 had not only not increased, but had actually diminished to the extent of about 3,000; and, therefore, that the same population which, in 1801, inhabited 17,000 houses, were, in 1851, crowded into 14,000 houses. In the parishes within the walls there had been the greatest decrease in the number of houses—2,776; but then there had been a corresponding diminution of population in these parishes to the extent of 19,000 souls. The result was that the average number of inhabitants of each house within the walls was the same in 1851 as it was in 1801,—namely, 7½ to

---

* See "London Shadows," 1854; and "Town Swamps and Social Bridges," 1859.

each house; but, in the City parishes without the walls, to which the poor have been driven by improvements effected in the metropolis, it appears that the houses have decreased in number about 300, while the population has increased by 19,000. Thus, while the proportion of inhabitants to each house in the inner parishes is 7½, in the outer parishes it has increased to 9⅔ in each house. The figures were given with reference to the year 1851; but, since then, great improvements have been going on in the City, the result of which has been to displace a very large number of the inhabitants.

In the Fleet valley, in the neighbourhood of Field Lane, about 1,000 houses were pulled down. These in the most miserable manner sheltered 4,000 families, comprising 12,000 persons. In single rooms in this neighbourhood we have found more than twenty persons,—men, women, and children, packed together;—in others, large families sleeping on a miserable pallet; and, although a considerable time has passed, we have not yet forgotten, nor are we likely to forget, the scenes which were met with on this now open spot. Close to the crowded dwellings along the banks of the pestilent Fleet were slaughter-yards, and offensive and unhealthy trades were carried on: in the dark and dingy streets were training-places and homes for thieves of the worst description: large groups of tenements swarming with people were undrained: dust-yards and other receptacles of filth were allowed to remain untouched for years, offending the air: the water-supply was neglected: the majority of the houses were dilapidated and without means of ventilation. A sample of the former condition of this district, although even this has been improved, may be seen in the labyrinth of courts situate near Clerkenwell Session-house. Although, as it is stated, 12,000 persons have been removed from this site, and inconvenienced, those who were acquainted with the conditions of it must rejoice that such a blot on the metropolis has been removed. It would have been well, however, if the corporate authorities of the city of London had then applied the large grant of money which was made some time previously for the erection of dwellings for the use of the industrious classes.

The resolution arrived at by the House of Lords must not be allowed to prevent the formation of metropolitan railways. It is clear that the immense and constantly increasing traffic of London cannot be much longer carried on with the present arrangements.

Railways must be carried forward, notwithstanding that many dwellings may have to be removed. Benefits, indeed, will follow the removal. All we ask for is, that a thought be given to the necessities of those persons who are turned out. According to laws made during the last few years, no houses within the metropolitan district can now be built without attention to drainage, paving, and other considerations: it must, therefore, be an advantage to the poor and industrious classes to be put into dwellings thus cared for, in lieu of the dens of which there are so many in older parts of the town.

At the present time London is in a remarkable state of change. In the very heart of the City the houses and places of business are putting on a new and much grander aspect. At the West End rows of dwellings are rising in thousands yearly, making the streets of fifty or sixty years of age look dwarfed and dingy. As these houses are finished, those which had been occupied by the prosperous portions of the community are left to people in poorer circumstances; and, by this process, buildings which, in Queen Anne's days, were inhabited by persons of fashion, are now each let in tenements to several tenants of less standing. In this there is evil, but upon the whole the advantages predominate.

We want a class of houses formed with especial reference to their inevitable occupation by more than one family; looking like ordinary residences, but with a separate entrance to each floor, and with separate conveniences. By-and-by, it may be hoped, old prejudices will be overcome, and numbers who now live in the courts, alleys, cellars, and garrets of the teeming hive London, may find their way, night and morning, to healthy rural villages, sub-suburbs, with the aid of the locomotive and far-seeing railway directors. Pending this, we fully agree with the instruction given by the House of Lords to the Select Committee on metropolitan railways,—"to inquire into and report upon the number of houses and of inhabitants likely to be removed by the works; and whether any provision has been made, or is required to be made, for diminishing the evils consequent on a large simultaneous displacement of the labouring population." We must go farther into the evils of overcrowding.

"Overcrowding" means want of pure air; and want of pure air means debility, continued fever, death, widowhood, orphanage, pauperism, and money-loss to the living. It should be needless now to give proof of its deadly doings. The often-told old story of the Calcutta Black-hole should alone have sufficed. The more recent incident in the Military Hospital at Versailles is less known.*

For several years, in a particular month, being about a week after the arrival of the then king at St. Cloud, there was a murderous epidemic of typhoid fever among the soldiers of the garrison. It never attacked the civil population, nor the officers, even of lowest grade. The cause was simply *overcrowding*. The garrison ordinarily consisted of 400 or 500 men; but when the then king came, the number was increased to 1,200. The men were in consequence closely packed in small rooms, and fever and death came at once amongst them. The non-commissioned officers, better fed, and never sleeping more than two in one room, escaped.

In the metropolis, within the last dozen years, great improvements, in a sanitary point of view, have been effected, legislation and public opinion having been brought to bear on the subject. As regards the particular evil, however, to which the writer would direct attention, it prevails still to an alarming and dangerous extent, and calls aloud for the application of such remedial measures as may be possible. Tracts have been cleared, new streets formed; hundreds of houses unfit for habitation destroyed; and though these steps must, on the whole, be viewed as most advantageous, it cannot be doubted that they have had the effect of filling some neighbourhoods more densely than before.

In the once notorious St. Giles's, model lodging-houses, churches, chapels, fine school-rooms, and other useful buildings, have taken the place of former dens, and have altered entirely the aspect of the locality. Even in most of the old houses which remain the conditions are changed. The common lodging-houses, which were formerly sinks of iniquity, where any number of persons were allowed to horde indiscriminately in filthy rooms, are now under the eye of the sanitary department of the police, and improved drainage,

* The following part of the chapter is the pith of a paper read by the Author at the London Congress of the Social Science Association. The evils remain unchanged.

water-supply, and breathing space are insisted on. Overcrowding still occurs in some of the houses; but we must look elsewhere for the greater part of the population formerly there. Some we may find in Seven Dials, in Great Wylde Street, and in the fearful alleys leading out of Drury Lane: people as evil, and living under conditions as bad in a sanitary point of view, as existed in the worst days of the "Rookery." Take, for instance, Lincoln Court, running from Drury Lane to Wylde Street; a place to which public attention was directed not very long ago by the discovery in it of a little child who, entitled to some fortune and position, had been cast into the river of vice flowing there by one who should have been a protector. The reflection, by the way, as to what this child would almost necessarily have become if it had been left to its fate in Lincoln Court, and what it may be with right teaching and under better circumstances, suggests a lesson and illustrates the value of a healthful and well-regulated home. In such a neighbourhood as this it is not easy to learn exactly the number of occupants in a house. There seems to be a fear amongst them of being meddled with, especially if Irish, which leads them to disguise the facts. It is certain, however, that the population of Lincoln Court is proportionally enormous. As far as could be ascertained, every room contains a separate family, if not more, and is thickly occupied. The inhabitants are of the dangerous classes. Haggard and drunken women, with every trace of womanhood blotted out, are in the pathway; and there are swarms of children, some trained to begging, and others, it may be feared, to worse. In the majority of the houses the rooms are small, and the staircases are narrow and without ventilation. In two of them it was admitted that more than thirty-five persons lived in each; but it would probably be nearer truth to say that each house of eight rooms contains, on an average, including children, forty-five persons; and as there are twenty-one houses, we have here perhaps 945 persons of the worst class pent up, to their own destruction and the danger of the public. In one small room were a man and his wife and six prostitutes, who were set forth as their daughters, but could not be so. Some scenes here witnessed could not be described. Re-examining this place in November of the present year (1863), the overcrowding seemed even more excessive than before.

Evidences of overcrowding turn up from time to time where they are not looked for. Not long ago a child was found dead in Brownlow Street; and on inquiry, it was learnt that the mother (a widow) and six children slept in one bed, in a small room. The death of the child was attributed to the bed-clothes. In such an atmosphere as a room so occupied must have, the vital power necessarily becomes weak; and to kill is easy. A dozen such cases have occurred since.

In a house of respectable appearance outside, we found a hole under the stairs made the sleeping-place for three persons, twenty-one, seventeen, and fourteen years of age (Fig. 8). It was intended originally for the reception of coals, is not more than four feet deep, and the height, of course, diminishes to nothing as the steps descend. When the door is closed there are only seven small gimlet-holes in the stairs for ventilation. Is it surprising that fevers break out under such circumstances? One is struck, sometimes, with the strange contrivances resorted to to meet the difficulty of want of room. Thus, in a model lodging-house for families, a father, who, with his wife and one child, occupies one room, has accommodated six of his nine other children the cross way on two camp-bedsteads, while three elder girls, one sixteen years old, sleep on a small bedstead near. The room is well ventilated and clean, but the same sort of stowing away is to be found in hundreds of cases under circumstances which render it deadly. In another room in the same building a wooden shelf has been contrived which can be pushed under the bedstead during the day, and drawn out at night to accommodate a pile of children. The illustrations of these incidents—Figs. 9 and 10—will speak for themselves.

Fig. 8.—A Bedroom under the Stairs.

In a respectable house not far from the last named, occupied by steady artisans and others, nine persons slept in one of the rooms (12 feet by 14 feet), —a father, mother, and seven children. Eleven shoemakers worked in the attics; and in each of the other five rooms there was a separate family. Scores of such cases of overcrowding, in what would seem to be decent houses, could be quoted; but the repetition might tire. No words, even aided by the pencil, can give a full idea of some of the dens which are occupied by a lower and different class: many born to evil, and without the power to rise; others the victims of more recent misfortunes or their own conduct. The world has still an interest in improving their condition; children as yet innocent cry aloud to be rescued from the otherwise inevitable gulf. In some places in the eastern districts, quite recently visited, ten,

Fig. 9.—Sleeping Accommodation for Nine Children.

eleven, and in more cases than one, fourteen persons were found occupying a single room. Nor can any authority interfere even when this occurs in a house let in tenements, so long as it be believed that the persons so lodging are members of the same family. The Nuisances Removal Act would seem to give power to remedy such cases, but practically it fails.

Seven hundred cubic feet are shown to be the smallest space, under ordinary arrangements, that will afford one person

Fig. 10.—Family Stowage: Nine Sleepers, besides Dog and Cat.

healthful sleeping-room. In apartments such as those last described, the occupants have not one-fifth of the required space.

D 2

In "London Shadows" we illustrated with engravings the contents of the houses in Charlotte's Buildings, Gray's-Inn Lane. The population here continues to be immense; and, although the drainage has been improved, the houses remain as black, as grimy, and as crowded as ever. In some of the dwellings the crowding is even greater. Close by are the houses known as Tyndall's Buildings, which have been made fit for healthful habitation by the Society for Improving the Condition of the Labouring Classes. These are let in apartments at moderate rents, and, nevertheless, are not full. It is most desirable that the real cause of this should be made clear. Formerly the houses there were crowded from the cellars to the attics, as those in Charlotte's Buildings and other places near still are: and now that the conveniences have been increased, that the water supply is improved, and other good arrangements have been made, rooms remain unlet. Various reasons may be suggested, but we must not pause to discuss them at any length.

Particular classes of the metropolitan population require peculiar accommodation. The costermongers, for example, who occupy Charlotte's Buildings, the neighbourhood of Leather Lane, and elsewhere, need room for their goods, barrows, and donkey-carts,—much space for small rent; and this is difficult to obtain in London. An attempt to meet their wants was made in the underground part of the Portpool Lane building, but it did not suit them to be separated from their goods; and so they continue where they can herd together as they like.

Hundreds of modern houses, built in decent suburban neighbourhoods as if for one family only, are made to contain several. The neat external appearance of many of them (one is shown Fig. 11) gives no suggestion of the dangerously-crowded state of the houses. A description of one in Bemerton Street, Caledonian Road, will be more truthful. The basement below the level of the street contains in the front room an old man and his wife; in the back room, two lodgers. In the parlours, there are a man and his wife and eight children. On the first floor, a man and his wife and infant; two girls, sixteen and eighteen years of age, and occasionally their mother,—all in the front room; and in the small back room, two women, a girl, and two young children. On the second floor, a father, mother, two grown-up sons, an infant, and a brood of rabbits. Two women and two boys in the back room make the whole population of the house thirty-four. In the next house there are thirty-three persons similarly divided. In a street to the westward matters are even worse The houses, moreover, are altogether unsuited to the use they are put to. Ventilation is not attended to; the drains get out of order, the "traps" are destroyed, and the atmosphere is poison.

In some old houses, in the St. Luke's district, for further example, the houses being built back to back there is no current of air.

In one house, with staircase in the centre, there were in the four small rooms on each side of it, forty persons in the day time. How many there may be at night cannot be said. The atmosphere on the staircase was sickening.

The Act for Regulating Common Lodging-houses has worked well: fevers have ceased to infest them; and the manners even of those frequenting them, it is said, especially with reference to the provinces, are

Fig. 11.—A Modern House with Thirty-four Occupants.

much improved. The Act nowhere defines the class of buildings intended to be designated as common lodging-houses, and a very limited application of it was made. We cannot avoid the conviction that its powers should be further applied: that all houses let in tenements should be registered, inspected, and regulated. It might be desirable to limit the application to houses let to more than two families, but this would be for consideration. Competent inspection and restriction as to the number of occupants in a given space are absolutely necessary. It should be no answer to the requirement of a certain cubical space for each occupier, that the financial resources of the parties would not admit of it. A man is not permitted to poison with prussic acid those who are dependent on him because he is poor; neither should he be allowed on that ground to kill them with bad air, and set up a fever-still for the benefit of his neighbours. "An Englishman's house is his castle" is a good saying, but surely it should not protect the ill-doer. Prejudices should be met as far as might be practicable; and if the duty of inspection were confided to the same department that now attends to common lodging-houses, it might be desirable that the officers employed should wear a distinctive dress, that their business at a man's house should at once be seen. Moreover, they should possess special knowledge and aptitude. It appears certain that typhoid fevers not long ago were destructive of life beyond former experience, and that, too, not so much in the dwellings of the poor as in those of a higher class. It is equally clear to all who have well considered the subject, that these diseases result from the neglect of sanitary law, or, at any rate, are spread by it. The parish inspector, the medical officer of health, and the sanitary police, have been at work in the courts and alleys, crowded back-slums, and common lodging-houses; and have effected great improvements in many quarters,—lessening the prevalence of disease. It is not too much to say that the inspection by competent persons, armed with certain powers, of the town and suburban dwellings of all classes, nay of dwellings in the country too, would be productive of the greatest advantage.

It is known that people are made ill and die from preventable causes. Endeavours, then, should surely be made to prevent them. An inquest is held touching deaths that occur through poison, or violence, or accident. We know that thousands of persons die as surely through sanitary ignorance, and neglect, wilful or otherwise, of sanitary laws. If inquiry were made in such cases, great advantages would result. At least, the buildings in which deaths have occurred from this known class of diseases, and the circumstances attending the deaths, should be investigated. It is not too much to assert that, in a large proportion of the cases where several members of a family have been swept away by zymotic disease, the proximate cause might be discovered by careful inspection on the part of qualified investigators. The assertion on the part of the occupiers, that there is nothing wrong about the house, and that it is perfectly healthy, is worth nothing. Custom blunts perception; and ignorance does not perceive. In a room over a stable in Baker Mews, Portman Square, three children died in less than three months. The briefest examination showed a bed-room without ventilation; a closet ill-placed; and the access of evil odours from below. With respect to a house wherein some fatal cases of diphtheria had occurred, it was asserted by some who ought to have known better, that there were no obvious reasons why the house should be unhealthy—the neighbourhood was open: the doctor had found no fault. On a personal examination, what was seen? The sketch Fig. 12 will show. An outhouse nearly filled with vegetable refuse; two water-closets in the house left without any but an accidental supply of water, through a disarrangement of the cistern that had not been attended to; an overflow of water from the cistern to saturate the dust-bin and vegetable refuse; and, to make matters still worse, a choked drain (B) which brought the soil back into the yard. Could such blindness be imagined? This is no invention, but a faithful picture. Scores of such cases could be given from our own experience.

Fig. 12.—Healthful Condition of a House in Islington.

In a house not far from that last mentioned, the child of working people was carried off in a day and a half by the same disease. We found that the parents occupied a small room in a house let to lodgers. In the basement, damp and unwholesome, were two families of costermongers, who at night kept fish and other offensive matter in the rooms. Here were dogs, cats, children, and dirt. In one room above them lived a shoemaker, wife, and son; in the back room a large family; and separate families in each of the four rooms above; one of the rooms including also, as is often the case, a number of rabbits. The atmosphere was offensive. The dust-bin was without cover, and the "closet," necessarily inadequate, was at the foot of the stairs. None need wonder that disease visits such a house. If intelligent inquiry were oftener made, cause and effect would become more widely recognized.

There was a house in the Old Kent Road, recently pulled down, where cholera, fever, and diphtheria had at different times been visitors, and in which many deaths occurred. Will any one say that power of inspection was not needed in this case? The house looked pleasant, as the sketch (Fig. 13) will suggest; but it was surrounded with a horrid ditch, and had

Fig. 13.—A Pestilent Suburban Cottage.

a stagnant pool behind. We give these facts to strengthen the claim for a power of inspection in respect of overcrowding.

Amongst the causes which lead to the evil we are deploring, we must not overlook the gradual increase of children, while, in the case of the labouring man, the income mostly remains the same. The want of providence on the part of such men is often commented on with good intentions. But, while admitting that better use might be made of their income in many instances, we must not omit to remember the cost of living in London, especially with a large family of children, and that thousands of these men are regular subscribers to benefit trade societies and other associations for providing aid in the event of sickness, accident, or death. The sum thus laid by is, in the gross, enormous. As the children increase in number, the wife is prevented from adding by her earnings to the income, and many years must elapse before the children can be put to work. To this class, often thus driven to evil lodgings, the occasional inspection of dwellings by authorized competent persons would be an immense advantage,—a saving of money, a saving of life and health! A consideration of their circumstances, moreover, suggests the importance of lessening the cost of wholesome and comfortable lodgings by all practicable means. Machinery might be brought to bear in carrying out this view to a greater extent than has yet been attempted. As boats of a particular set of patterns may be built in numbers at an immensely reduced cost, so might houses be cheaply built for the struggling classes. The increased value of land in towns forms necessarily a material item, and seems to necessitate building *high* instead of building *wide*. The ground-rent for two sets of apartments would remain the same for say five sets formed one over another; and while, in the one case, it would be oppressive, or even insurmountable, might in the other offer no difficulty. Houses, moreover, must be built with a view to receiving a number of families, and not, as now, as if for one family only; and those assessments which militate against such arrangements should at once be reconsidered.

It is not alone in sleeping-rooms that overcrowding to a dangerous extent still occurs. Look into the work-rooms in many parts of the metropolis, and you will find them filled to far over danger point. Artificial flower-making, formerly practised mainly by individuals at their own homes, is now a great trade carried on by persons who employ large numbers of women and children for the most part crammed into small rooms where healthful existence is impossible. In an upper room in Oxford Street, not ten feet square, twenty delicate young women may be seen closely shut up, pursuing this occupation; and there, when business is pressing, they remain at times from eight o'clock in the morning till twelve at night. In another house nearly every room is filled in a similar manner. Here is a drawing of one made on the spot (Fig. 14). Many of the work-rooms of fashionable milliners are similarly overcrowded, as are those where young girls are engaged in book-stitching. Take as an example, a house in Fleet Street, looked at not long ago. The passage is narrow; a door in it shuts with a spring; the staircase is confined, and without ventilation; the atmosphere is steamy, and smells of glue; ascending, it is seen that all the doors shut with springs. In the first room looked into forty young women and girls were sorting and stitching books. There was a stove, but no ventilation. Without going further into details, there were more than 200 persons in that house, pent up without provision of the first necessity of life, pure air. Poor creatures so placed are being slowly slain.

Fig. 14.—Artificial-flower Makers: Blighting the Buds.

Breathing space is at all times necessary, and more especially when sickness or death is in the house. Yet what do we often see? Amongst the London Irish, when death occurs, the neighbours and friends assemble in large numbers to poison one another. We have seen a small unventilated room thronged with neighbours about the body of a child arrayed in flowers and ribbons, lighted by large candles in massive candlesticks borrowed from the publican (Fig. 15). During the time of sickness, too, it is the practice to crowd the room. We have heard of thirteen persons round a sick woman in a small back parlour used as a bed-room. Here is a sketch of it (Fig. 16).

In several parts of London, persons employed in making cheap clothing are boxed up in crowds, in a manner that could not be guessed by those who have not made a personal examination. In a small room not large enough for three, twenty-five tailors may be seen. In another, boys and women strive to get a living in a death-giving atmosphere. Shoemakers are often as ill

STICKING TO THE LAST. 43

placed. In wretched apartments in an ill-drained house may be found men and boys huddled together without room to breathe; where, as one so placed

Fig. 15.—" Waking" the Dead and Killing the Living.   *Fig. 16.—A Very Sick Room.*

remarked grimly, while they are drawing the strings of misery, they are "closing up" their own lives. Fig. 17 shows a shoemaker's workshop in

Fig. 17.—A Shoemaker's Workshop: more Care for the "Soles" than the Bodies.

Somers Town. Other trades, such as cap and bonnet makers, trimmers, blonde-joiners, &c., to which we have looked with some little care, are forced in many places to do much the same thing. The extent of suffering entailed, and the loss to the community, it would be difficult to calculate. It is not simply a duty and an act of justice on the part of employers to provide wholesome workplaces for their people, but advantageous even, pecuniarily, in the long run. These inducements, however, do not prove to be sufficient, and it is time, therefore, that legislation should be tried. Interference is needed for thousands of persons, especially young females — the debilitated mothers *in posse*, should they live, of our future population. In our infant schools, too, where incalculable mischief is done by overcrowding, it is greatly required. Fig. 18 represents an overfilled example.

Fig. 18.—Murdering the Innocents.

This is no slight matter of which we are speaking. The evil is sapping the strength of the land; and concerns as well the political economist as the philanthropist and the Christian.

When these statements were made at the Social Science Congress, they appeared to excite much attention, and it was hoped that they might lead to such legislation on the subject as is desired. The *Times*, commenting on it in a forcible leading article, remarks :—

"We are not in a position to say whether a more vigorous application of the existing law might not abate these evils, but we quite agree with Mr. Godwin that, by some means or other, it is high time to check them. It is vain to trust entirely to the vigilance of individuals in such a case. The wretched fathers of families who rent this class of lodgings think of nothing but the smallness of their wages, the cost of living, and the increasing number of their children. They could not make terms for the improvement of their ventilation, even if they saw the want of it. The fact is, however, that they do not. 'Custom blunts perception, and ignorance does not perceive.' Few of the other conditions of health can be violated without suffering more or less palpable. Insufficiency of food makes itself felt through the pangs of hunger, and even unwholesome food occasions painful symptoms which cannot be overlooked or mistaken. But most men live in the atmospheric ocean which surrounds us without being conscious of its quality. Bad air does not burn, or drown, or sensibly affect him who inhales it; it only causes life to flow at a low ebb, takes the edge off the appetite, impairs the digestion, depresses the spirits, weakens the muscular power, deprives sleep of its refreshing influence, and predisposes to mortal disease. All these are occult effects, and even educated persons have not yet learned to trace them to their causes."

And again :—

"The Legislature has a right to interfere at least on behalf of the innocent victims of their landlords' or neighbours' negligence; and, by fixing a statutable *minimum* of breathing room in cases where such protection shall be proved to be most needed, may gradually enlighten public opinion on this subject."

The *Times* is less hopeful than we are as to what may be done by personal efforts :—

"A radical change of ideas and habits [says that journal] is not the work of one session or of one generation. To eradicate the superstitious notions that diseases come by chance, or are sent by an arbitrary Providence; to implant a faith in the power of man to preserve his own health, and procure for himself the prospect of length of days; to persuade the mass of mankind that the sins of the fathers are here visited on the children, and that a want of pure air produces not only fever and loss of wages, but a sickly offspring—this is a task which the statesman cannot undertake, and which the philanthropist will hardly achieve before the dawn of an educational millennium."

We look for it long before. We have already seen great changes in public opinion on the matter, and shall see greater, if those who know what is right persevere in their endeavours, and a knowledge of sanitary laws be widely spread.

The *Morning Advertiser* draws attention to the same subject in two leaders :—

"There are evils," says the editor, "which accompany 'overcrowding' with which it is clearly the right and the duty of the Legislature to interfere. Mr. Godwin speaks of a locality —one out of many—in which the drains are out of order, the 'traps' destroyed, and the atmosphere pestilential. Surely, at least, we should have inspection here. 'The Act,' he says, 'for regulating common lodging-houses has worked well; fevers have ceased to infest them, and the manners even of those frequenting them, it is said, especially with reference to the provinces, are much improved. The Act nowhere defines the class of buildings intended to be designated as common lodging-houses, and a very limited application of it was made. I cannot avoid the conviction that its powers should be farther applied; that all houses let in tenements should be registered, inspected, and regulated.'

"We quite agree with the writer. We believe that this extension of the powers of the Common Lodging-houses Act is the first essential step towards the abatement of an evil which he says, justly, 'concerns as well the political economist as the philanthropist and the Christian.' The overcrowding of our great towns is a reproach to all three. It is a waste of power; demoralizing to human nature; and a sin against charity. When Mr. Godwin's paper has been carefully read and pondered, let our readers take this caution with them :— that it is only an indication, and, careful and painstaking as it is, only a very faint indication, of the degraded condition in which tens of thousands of our fellow-creatures are living,— a condition so debased, and so surrounded with depraving influences, that morality and Christianity become under its influences almost impossibilities. But now, to turn this dissertation to profit, how long are we to suffer this evil? *Quousque tandem?* Surely the Social Science Congress will not have pleaded in vain in the British metropolis for the emancipation of a vast population from the thraldom of moral and physical debasement."

The subdivision of labour in artificial-flower making to which we have referred is considerable. The wire which forms the stems has to be covered with paper of a green, yellow, brown, or other suitable tint. The leaves have to be cut, stamped, and shaded. These have to be fixed in the proper position. The pistils and similar portions are usually purchased from those who deal in the materials required by the flower-makers; but the other parts of the flowers have to be stamped out, and stitched or pasted in the right place. Very little girls can perform some of the work without much teaching or practice; so that, in order to keep pace with competition, young children of from six to eight years of age are engaged at wages of about 1s. 6d. or 2s. a week. Some of these eventually become artificial florists themselves, and in consequence the number of those engaged in this branch rapidly increases.

In several instances which have come under our notice, the girls are pent up in space inconsistent with healthful existence: ventilation is neglected, and there is, besides, the evil of the poisonous materials with which they work. In one of those places, nearly every room in the house was filled with groups of young girls, superintended by forewomen; and although, in some cases, kindness is shown by the employers to their workpeople, in others there is a most reprehensible system pursued, so that, when business is pressing, young children and delicate girls are kept at work, with but short intermission, from eight o'clock in the morning till twelve at night.

Such a state of things as this should not be permitted. The laws should protect those who cannot protect themselves.

CHAPTER V.

ST. LUKE'S—WHETSTONE PARK—ST. CLEMENT'S DANES—WATER.

MANY have heard of the benighted state of Golden Lane, St. Luke's, and of its neighbourhood, from the often-repeated appeals of Mr. Rogers, the late incumbent of St. Bartholomew's district; while others of an antiquarian turn may remember accounts of the time when Golden Lane and its surrounding parts were a fashionable locality,—when the theatre of Queen Elizabeth's days existed, and green trees and fields stood in the place of the endless rows of houses and other buildings which now exist. Generally, however, except to the immediate dwellers, little is known of this, perhaps one of the poorest and most neglected parts of the metropolis. It is most densely populated. From Old Street, an important thoroughfare (" the old highway from Aldersgate for the north-east parts of England, before Bishopsgate was built "), branch on both sides many streets, most of them narrow: from these run courts and alleys teeming with an immense population, chiefly in a poor and forlorn condition. Strange and dreary is the appearance of these avenues, in spite of the bright sunshine. Let us, however, make a more minute examination,—walk to Golden Lane and its tributaries, and see how these are cared for. Leading from the lane in Cherry-tree Court, a place barely four feet in width, are seven houses on one side and a high wall on the other. Externally the houses are not in bad repair, but within their dirty and dilapidated state is remarkable. In one small back room were a little boy nine years of age, and a girl some years younger, who had scarcely a rag of covering on them; there were two other children out, we were told, working in the street. Those at home crouching over the fire were altogether uninstructed. Their mother made a living in the markets, they said, and their father had run away. A wretched bundle of rags in a corner served for bedding. In a back yard, unpaved and broken, was the overflow water from cesspools, the closet was stopped and in bad order: there was only surface-drainage, and that of an incomplete description, and yet every room of these premises was occupied by a family, some of them consisting of seven, eight, or nine persons. In most of the houses the water "ran short;" on Sundays "the water is turned on for about five minutes, but sometimes it does not reach them." We trust that the day is not far distant when compulsory drainage, *thoroughly carried out,* will be made a rule in connexion with the dwellings of the poor. Remarking that the scavengers perform their duty very badly, we pass on to Hartshorn Court, a singular locality, which, with the parts adjoining, is inhabited to a great extent by thieves and the most dangerous characters. This is the entrance to a labyrinth of courts which, like the intricate workings of a Gloucestershire iron-mine, lead in all manner of curious and mysterious directions. In front of five houses is a kind of square, which formerly has probably been occupied as gardens; here swarms of children peer curiously out, neglected little creatures, so forlorn, so helpless for good, that the first impulse is to ask—What is to become of them? What path in life, according to present arrangements, are they fitted for? What, except by chance, is there for them but beggary or the prison?

The houses mentioned are single houses (one room deep), without any openings at the back. Like those previously alluded to, these dwellings are, so far as exterior is concerned, not in bad repair, but anything worse than the interiors cannot be easily imagined. Let us step up one of the dark narrow staircases: in one room, on the door being opened, a man had risen hastily from his bed; a strong active-looking woman was there, and from the mass of rags swarmed out a number of children (it was about ten o'clock in the morning). Few could look at these helpless things without an aching heart: the faces, not ill-shaped, were massed with dirt, and they had scarcely a rag of covering upon them; there was no furniture in the room, the window was plastered with mud; and the floor, although an able woman was there, had probably not been washed for months. The tenant complained of the landlord's neglect. Modestly, we ventured to hint that if the wife were to clean the broken glass of the windows and, maybe, give the floor a good washing, when the landlord next called for his rent he would be so much astonished at the contrast, that he would set some one to put the walls in order immediately.

In all parts there are apartments in a similar condition; no attempt is made at ventilation, there are no back windows, no openings to the roof; dirt and crowding, particularly in the upper rooms, produce an atmosphere unpleasant and unwholesome.

For a population of ninety and more persons, there are only two closets, in a most filthy condition, over which is the water-tank. How can people be clean or decent under such circumstances? Refuse is left in all directions, and the roadways, in bad weather, are deep with poisonous and stagnant water. Turning sharply to the left of the *play-ground*, we come to Little Cheapside. In this and other places, close by, may be seen groups of houses without proper accommodation; even the surface drainage is not good; the pavement is abominable, and the whole of the place around polluted with cesspools.

We look into many houses and tenements, and hundreds might be described, so much alike, that an account of one would almost serve for the others. Range after range of houses, badly constructed; the roads and yards unpaved, or patched in such a manner as to be of but little use; the soil saturated with the most unwholesome matters to a considerable depth; room after room, to the extent of thousands, all loaded with dirt; the same pictures of broken ceilings and walls; half-naked and half-fed children; old witch-like women, crouching by the fire-grates; men entirely or partially drunk, lying on shavings, or rags, on the floors, nearly all without furniture,—these form the picture. Without fully particularizing, we will jot down a few characteristic features.

Twelve houses constitute a narrow court, sunk below the regular surface; there are two closets only for all these—there was, a short time ago, only one. Here dwell persons who might give information respecting missing dogs. Gladly do we escape from the din of barking brutes, and the unpleasant physiognomy of the inhabitants. Let us proceed to a fresh spot. Another narrow court, in which are several houses, having cellars below them. In passing, bad as have been the smells already experienced, they seem faint in comparison with that which rises from the gratings. By means of the open window above one of these we see a sickly woman, and a child lying in a corner still more sadly stricken. This is not to be wondered at, for, descending into the cellar there will be found an untrapped and dirty closet (Fig. 19), the water-cask close to it, and an accumulation of refuse, which had been allowed by the scavengers to remain for six months. Up the staircase, by the crevices of the floors, through the open windows, the fever-bringing gases find their way into the rooms.

Let us make another sketch. It is a square room, the walls of which we can touch either way by stretching out the arms; close to the window is a closet, untrapped, and a cesspool; the unpaved little yard is overflowing (Fig. 20). In a room like this a family of six persons may be found. Such is

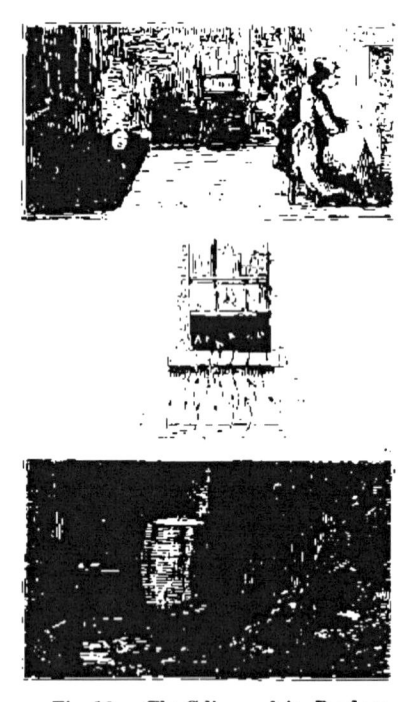

Fig. 19.—The Cellar and its Produce.   *Fig. 20.—A Pleasant Garden.*

the unpleasant effluvium which arises from the back premises, that the tenants cannot open the window, particularly in summer time.

We peeped into another interior, dirty beyond description,—a man on the floor asleep,—the children out at *work*, which probably consists in turning "catherine-wheels," or some less honest employment. Onions and other vegetables are lying about to be made ready for sale. The atmosphere, if possible, is worse than usual; the ceiling and walls are black as the back of a

ST. LUKE'S.

chimney. The fireplace and chimney project, and a large portion of the upper part of the brickwork has been removed; so that the smoke spreads over the walls and roof (Fig. 21.) On the person here waking up, and some remarks having been made that it would be better for health to have a little ventilation, he at once said, "Certainly," and then lifted out the window-frame bodily, and placed it against the wall.

Words and sketches fail to give an idea of what is going on around us. Nothing but a personal inspection can afford a just notion of the state in which these poor and often ignorant people are allowed to be. In one small room, without any separation, live nine grown-up persons and two children,—eleven in all. There are the mother, married sons and daughters, and the children, all living in this promiscuous manner.

In some parishes the sanitary arrangements are much more effective than in others. In St. Luke's, the relative state is not good. When saying so, however, we must not omit

Fig. 21.—Home Comfort.

to add that the district is overrun by the poor, and that the chief body of ratepayers are but ill able to meet the heavy demands made upon them. Still there are matters which depend on sanitary inspection, and where the forcing of the proprietors of houses to do what is right might not only be beneficial to the inhabitants, but, by preserving health, be a saving in the poorrates. We will now look at one more group of houses. In an ill-paved yard is a closet, the cesspool is overflowing, the surplus standing in pools, and running down the gutter and into a smith's premises. The smith says that at times he is flooded with it, and that at the last attack of cholera, himself and two sons were in the hospital ill with this disease at the same time, and that deaths happened in the adjoining houses. "But see," said an old man, "the state of the place a little way back. I have a large family, which in a measure forces me to live in such a hole. Look at the house adjoining; a drunken man, if he fell, would knock the wall out; there are two closets overflowing, the dust and other refuse are inundated; close to this is the window of my bedroom; no one would imagine what a horrible atmosphere we breathe." Mr. Rogers' schools, and a harbour for the houseless in Playhouse Yard, are bright spots in this darkness.

Various interests are antagonistic to the rapid improvement of the dwellings of the poor to which we have referred; but the statesman will be a benefactor to his country who will with firmness and vigour grapple with the monstrous evils that so much need remedy. The important points to be aimed at are, we repeat,—

1st. Power to overlook houses let in tenements, and to enforce necessary improvements.

2nd. The power of preventing the letting of such houses to more persons than the amount of space will healthfully admit of.

3rd. The establishment of Ragged Schools, and the provision of means for the removal of the youth of both sexes from situations which leave no hope.

Metropolitan medical officers of health have, from time to time, urged the necessity for more attention to be paid, particularly in the summer months, to the condition of mews; and it was recommended that some plan should be arranged for the regular removal of the refuse, and the prevention of those accumulations which spread an impure atmosphere to some distance around. It was with surprise we noticed that a deputation, consisting of Alderman Salomons and others, had waited upon the Chief Commissioner of Works, for the purpose of opposing this wholesome proposition.

These mews are mostly of considerable extent, formed behind rows of large and fashionable houses, by which they are hidden from the general view; and the circumstance of their being thus built in increases the necessity for the use of every sanitary precaution, not only for the preservation of the health of those dwelling around, but of that of the animals which are lodged in the mews, and the men, women, and children who dwell, in numbers of cases, above them. During the winter months, when those engaged in the culture of land are at leisure, the refuse of stables and, indeed, every other description of decomposing matter, is eagerly sought for and readily removed. In the summer and autumn time, when there is in crowded towns the greater need for attention to the purity of the atmosphere, farmers, being engaged in their fields, do not care so much as at other times for manure, which is often allowed to remain unmoved. Those dwelling in well-conditioned houses near mews know the unpleasant smells, particularly when the atmosphere is hot and dense, which come from them; and the evil gases they generate cause, no doubt, many attacks of sickness for which it seems otherwise difficult to account. We sketch a mews near Russell Square (Fig. 22).

Fig. 22.—A Mews near Russell Square.

In most of the courts and narrow passages which are teeming with human life, the manner of the water-supply, notwithstanding all that has been said, is in most respects not better than it was seven or eight years ago. In the afternoon, those who pass that way may see, on looking up the narrow entrances of these courts, crowds of women and children; and, on making a closer inspection, will find that there are from twenty-five to thirty people, provided with bottles, pails, tubs, tea-kettles, broken jugs, and other vessels. These people will tell you that they have not a drop of water in their houses;

if you seem to doubt their word, they will take you to their miserable homes and show you that this is the fact; and you might examine twenty of these rooms, at from two till past three o'clock, and not find any water in nineteen of them. The groups to which we have referred are waiting for the turncock to make the water flow from the main; and it is necessary to be in time, for many want to be supplied, and it runs only twenty minutes. At length the water issues from a lead pipe of not more than half an inch in diameter; so small is the stream, that it is difficult, even for those who are provided with proper vessels, to get what is wanted; and some are so ill off in this respect, that they are not able to collect more than a gallon of water (Fig. 23). How can the skin, the clothes, or the rooms be kept decent under such circumstances? At the best, these arrangements are bad; for, as our readers know, even if there be enough water taken into these apartments, the atmosphere is so vitiated that the water is spoiled and rendered unwholesome in a few hours. Even the placing of cisterns in such situations is not good, for the air is loaded with pollution.

Fig. 23.—Water-Supply,—no Supply. Fryingpan Alley, Clerkenwell.

It is surely time that the disgraceful state of affairs to which we have pointed was ended; the loss, if any, to the water companies, by adopting better arrangements, would not be felt; it is, however, more the duty of those who own and let these premises to ensure a proper supply of water by the payment to the companies of a sufficient sum for the purpose. Drinking-fountains have been placed in our highways and byways; but in some of the dark courts and lanes pure water is as scarce as it is on board an emigrant ship during a long voyage. Careful inquiry, in various districts, shows us that this evil is extensive, and that it needs a speedy remedy. We trust *soon* that with the poor inhabitants of these courts their "water shall be sure." Sickness and death attend sanitary derangements as surely as the darkness follows the daylight. Unfortunately, sanitary principles are not so well understood as they ought to be. There are, moreover, instances in which even those who have studied this important matter are deceived, and are unable to account for derangements of health which are evidently caused by impurity of the atmosphere. A case which illustrates this in a most striking manner has been lately brought under our notice.

In a street in the north of London which is composed of small cottage houses, there has been a great deal of illness. The dwellings are occupied by persons who are employed on a railway, at the post-office, and elsewhere; most of whom have large families of children; and for years past the place has been well known by the neighbouring medical men. Fevers and low pining sickness have been prevalent; and in the case of one house the medical attendant declared that the only mode of saving the children's lives was for the parents to move them away. In other houses, where the inmates were in comfortable circumstances, there have been serious and fatal attacks of illness; and it is satisfactory to note that in several instances the drain-pipe layer has followed the attendance of the doctor with good effect.

In the house marked A on the little plan we have engraved (Fig. 24), a child had been for more than a month suffering from a low intermittent fever, which up to the time of writing had baffled the power of medicine,—the child continuing to get weaker daily. Some time before there had been a derangement of the drains, which had been set right; and, although examination was then made, there was no suspicion of the existence of a cesspool near. In the house B, the last tenant, who did his work at home, constantly complained of being ill, and left the place in consequence. Now the children there are ill of whooping-cough and measles. In the house C, nearly all the children are ill, and the doctor has been in frequent attendance for some time past. In the back room D, two children died of whooping-cough and debility, and were buried on the same day.

In consequence of all this sickness, further examination of the drainage was made, and a large cesspool was found in the rear of the house B. On raising the broken woodwork of the floor of the wash-house, a large pit completely filled with poisonous refuse was seen. There was no brick arch over the cesspool—no cover except the cracked boards, which were so much decayed that it seemed providential the children who were in the habit of playing over the pit had not fallen into it. Into this cesspool several houses to the northward drained; and a reference to the ground-plan will show how close this pestilential collection is to the room in which the two children died. The cesspool is marked E, and the closets of the other houses F. These are untrapped, and not properly supplied with water.

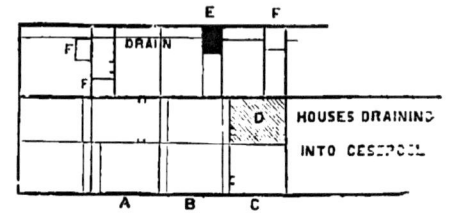

Fig. 24.—Sickness in the Washouse, and Why?

There is undoubtedly here sufficient proximate cause for disease; and we have mentioned the circumstance in the hope that this experience may lead others, in doubtful cases of sickness, to make careful sanitary investigation, and obtain the removal of matters which are often dangerous to a whole neighbourhood. If we can make the public connect cause and effect in this matter of health, we shall have done something towards amendment.

CHAPTER VI.

THE THAMES.—WORK TO BE DONE.

THERE is a big giant lying in the sludge who is about to be slain. A mighty river runs through the heart of the richest city in the world. This stream, instead of bringing health and healing on its bright waters to the three millions of inhabitants living around its banks, is suffered to become so foul by the discharge of common sewers into it, that at certain seasons it is as a rotting sea, where "a thousand thousand slimy things" disport themselves, and whence is wafted into the crowded streets an odour that even the long-suffering statesmen, legislating in the palace on its shore, have pronounced unbearable. If we were to hear of this circumstance in connexion with some foreign city—St. Petersburgh, Constantinople, or Damascus—we should exclaim, "Benighted people! they should bargain with English enterprise and English energy, and their river would be purified in a month!" But the current rendered so offensive—thus converted into a *cloaca maxima*—is no other than the Thames: it flows past regal Windsor and through commercial London.

"Thames, the most loved of all the Ocean's sons,"

has got into a sad mess: dirty is his bed, and squalid are his banks. We have made a sketch (Fig. 25) to show what is the actual aspect, on the river, of—

———"the glorious city,
Which holds the fair, the rich, the gay, the witty."

However, the work of improvement has been commenced, and in the course of time we shall have a clearly-defined and substantial margin to our great river, with a roadway, extending on the north from Westminster to the Tower, and on the south throughout such a distance as will afford the required convenience and prevent the damage which is caused by floods. In arranging this matter there should be no half measures; nothing short of the best.

Besides other advantages, the new embankment shadows forth the prospect of a remedy for the unsightly unarchitectural appearance which the banks of the most populous, wealthy, and prosperous City in the world now offer. At the present time, when passing along the Thames from the Houses of Parliament towards the east, there is, landward, but little to gratify

Fig. 25.—The North Bank of the Thames: East of Blackfriars Bridge.

the eye. On a near view, the dilapidated condition of some places, the waste of space, and the inconvenience of such a neighbourhood for business, would surprise those who, not being acquainted with this locality, might pay it a visit. Denham sings—

> "In that blest moment, from his oozy bed,
> Old Father Thames advanced his reverend head;
> His tresses dripp'd with dews, and o'er the stream
> His shining horns diffused a golden gleam;
> Graved on his urn appear'd the moon that guides
> His swelling waters and alternate tides;
> The figured streams in waves of silver roll'd,
> And on their banks Augusta rose in gold."

Our sketch shows how Augusta in this quarter has been tarnished.

In making the embankment, advantage should be taken of the objects of beauty and interest which remain along the metropolitan portion of the Thames. York Gate should not be hidden. Waterloo Bridge, with the land approaches in connexion with Somerset House, is very fine, and might be suggestive for the continuation of new works. The view at present is chaotic. Byron scarcely exaggerates :—

> "A mighty maze of bricks and smoke and shipping,
>   Dirty and dusky, but wide as eye
> Could reach, with here and there a sail just skipping
>   In sight, then lost amidst the forestry
> Of masts ; a wilderness of steeples peeping
>   On tiptoe through their sea-coal canopy ;
> A huge dun cupola, like a foolscap crown
> On a fool's head—and there is London town."

Year after year the water views of St. Paul's have been more damaged by the erection of shapeless blocks of buildings; and so the masterpiece of Sir Christopher Wren, the chief glory of the city, has been hidden from points of sight where its beauty would be most apparent.

We long earnestly to see the works carried on, and expect that the changes and improvements on the banks of the Thames will be so great and rapid, that in a few years our illustration will be looked at with wonder and doubt. When the health and pleasure giving river, transformed into a pestilent sewer, has been brought back to its original condition, and that which befouled it and plagued the nostrils of the town has been made to fertilize the earth and minister to man's support, Londoners will indeed have done a work of mark.

Let us look elsewhere. We find, not only in the metropolis and its suburbs, but in country towns, and more frequently still in villages, houses built upon undrained land, without the slightest provision for sewerage. Here then, again, head and hands are needed. We know that the effluvia arising from the deposits that are necessarily made around such places, must so affect the air in the immediate and surrounding neighbourhood as to render it fruitful with fever and other epidemics, and we calmly suffer this state of things to continue. This disregard of drainage is the next enemy we must vanquish. There is already a force in the field against it. Local boards of health should obtain powers, and stringently insist upon proper means of drainage being afforded to every inhabited building: whether new or old; whether in remote or public places; whether occupied by a pauper or a peer. They should get powers, too, to look into all buildings let in tenements. Having disposed of these monster evils, we should have leisure to consider how many lives might be saved annually by the more general use of fireproof floors and staircases. The expense of these might be too considerable for small common houses; but no consideration of this kind should prevent the universal use of fireproof staircases in habitations of many stories. A glance at statistics shows us that the number of fires is on the increase. Who that has seen the pale figure of a human being at the window of a house on fire, wildly imploring rescue,—who that read the harrowing details of the burning of the Kildare Street Club-house in Dublin, when James Wilson Hughes, the bookkeeper, showed us what heroes live amongst us unknown, can have a doubt about the propriety of building all tall houses with fireproof staircases, and with proper arrangements for escape? In the construction of our houses generally, other great improvements are desirable: they are full of evils which wait to be conquered.

Then, in the matter of homes or harbours for our noble fleet, and the still more noble seamen therein employed, we have a large margin for improvement. The instance at Alderney, where the frigate *Emerald* was jammed hard and fast upon a hidden rock, in the very centre of the harbour, shows that we do not always take the trouble to learn whether we are enclosing a reef, or any other danger, in the bosom of our refuges from sea storms. We have diving-bells, we have dredging-machines, and we spend ungrudgingly many thousands of pounds weekly on our harbours and docks. When we are about to form a harbour, we must ascertain whether we shall have any enemies to contend against in its deep bed. And we should also take careful soundings of our existing harbours, to prevent the recurrence of danger similar to that which the ship we have named, with the two batteries of the 15th Brigade on board, so narrowly escaped. Then, too, we must form additional harbours of refuge, and more lighthouses, to render our seas, under Providence, as safe as our high roads.

Many of our provincial towns, wealthy and thriving, are in a discreditable state, and need thorough revision and improvement. Under the direction of the writer a number of these towns have been examined and reported on, in some cases with good practical results. The want of enlarged views in the management of our cities and towns is undeniable.

The poor, we have been assured, we shall have always with us. It well becomes us to do our utmost to lighten their lot. Sunshine was given alike to all, save the blind; and as its vivifying influence is now well understood, we should be resolute in securing its admission into all dwellings, more especially those of the poor and those intended for the sick! The repeal of the window-duty has left the matter entirely in the hands of the public. There is no reason why large and numerous windows should not permit the glorious sunrise, daylight, and sunset to flood into the meanest home. We are taught in a proverb to regard cleanliness as standing next among the virtues to godliness; and we all fully recognize the advantage of cleanliness in a class that it is the fashion to call "the great unwashed." But who, unless endowed with more than average energy and health, could be clean with no water, little light, and less air? So it behoves us to urge, and re-urge, the imperative necessity of seeing that all the children of Adam and Eve under the rule of our most gracious Queen are properly housed, allowed to breathe fresh air, and supplied with pure water. Not only those whose daily course is run in the dingy, melancholy back streets of the metropolis, or who are engaged in the various trades of our manufacturing cities, but field and farm workers and labourers of every description require protection, or instruction which would enable them to protect themselves.

In connexion with fatal cases of disease which have occurred in overcrowded dwellings,—the numerous forms of death produced by impure air,—we have made some inquiries respecting the obvious effects produced by overcrowding and the polluted air on the inhabitants of these places; and it may not be without useful results to mention some of the statements which have been made by the people themselves. In many of those small interiors where seven, eight, nine, ten, and even more persons sleep in a room, we hear of a heavy drowsiness, which renders old and young stupid and weak in the morning. Children lie like dead things until they are roused by the opening of doors and windows. There is a general complaint that, during the night, particularly towards the morning, the bodies of the inmates are covered with a clammy, unwholesome perspiration. Some said that, in the morning, the sweat ran in streams from their faces. First, this was hot; but on getting into the air it changed into large cold drops, which gradually declined in quantity until the skin became intensely cold and dry. This occurred even in tolerably mild weather. The nature of the water-supply prevents regular washing even of the face and hands; and in these situations, in nine cases out of ten, nothing more is thought of. We may readily judge how seriously these conditions must affect health. During some early visits recently made to East London, we found the state of some of the rooms to be shocking. The dirty bed-clothes were reeking with fumes; and, although it goes sorely against our inclination to make the comparison, it is the truth to say that, in some of these places, the human tenants suggested only the idea of decomposing vegetation. In one room six children had been washed in a dish in which there was about a quart of water; and this, by the renewed operation, instead of being a liquid, had become a semi-solid body. In some rooms, the ragged, black-looking bed-coverings had not been washed for months: one woman said that she had lived in a room for two years, and had found no opportunity for washing or drying her quilt or blanket. How can we wonder, then,—when we consider these arrangements, the density of the population of the houses, and their neglected and unsanitary state,—that fevers rage and multitudes of children die?

Model lodging-houses are essentially an institution of these latter days. If we made them a little less like factories and barracks, it would go far to give an air of home to them—a quality those experimentally erected can hardly be said to possess. As a suggestion for further consideration, we might inquire how far infant-schools and play-grounds in connexion with the lodging-houses for married people would be conducive to the general weal? But we must here leave our prospective sketch, though it be but washed in, and does not embrace half the subject. Our workhouses, hospitals, manufactories, and barracks, all offer evils to be conquered, and we have not said one word of the victories that wait to be achieved in the higher realms of architectural art. We must not merely get rid of the ugly, but we must set up what is handsome. This has something to do even with health.

CHAPTER VII.

DRURY LANE—HOUSES OF THE DANGEROUS CLASSES.

ON a recent warm Sunday night we passed down Drury Lane. There was no air stirring; the footways were full of women and children sitting and standing about the entrance to the various courts behind: there was nothing bright but the gin-shops, which were ablaze with gas, and were driving a roaring trade. The condition of the atmosphere was disagreeable everywhere; but on passing a narrow turning on the west side of the way, at the north end, called Ashlin's Place, the effluvium was sickening; and when led by the nose we passed down it, this became worse and worse. It was too dark to discover much of its condition, so we returned soon after, in the morning, when the accompanying sketch of a block of building in it was made (Fig. 26); a building which was doubtless erected before the advent of the Great Plague of 1665.

It is asserted with reference to that terrible pestilence, that the first case occurred in Drury Lane, opposite to the Coal Yard. Now this house, which is situated in Drury Lane, exactly opposite to the Coal Yard, is perhaps the very house in which the plague first showed itself. Without care for drainage or paving, it is not to be wondered at that in the parish of St. Giles-in-the-Fields the pestilence carried off so many that it was difficult to find room for the dead in the parish grave-yard; but it *is* a matter of surprise that, after two hundred years have gone by, during which knowledge has been constantly increasing, we should find, exactly on the spot which had such a notorious character in the past, the existence of precisely similar evils in the present.

The upper part of this structure is now ruinous, but it is not long since it was inhabited. All round it the houses are thickly populated, and persons in passing will wonder at a place seemingly useless being allowed to remain. A more close inspection will, however, show that, hidden and hoarded up, there are here, in the lower apartments, in darkness visible, a large number of cows, which supply various families with milk. Here, shut out from the daylight, and supplied with food which is unnatural to the animals, they are kept for long periods without proper air or exercise. It is impossible that the produce of these unfortunate brutes can be wholesome. It is, moreover, certain that the bad smells which come from this and other places similarly situated are injurious to the health of those dwelling near. There are two gully-holes in this court, not more than four yards apart, which are most offensive. We were, however, told that, bad as the condition of this spot now is, it is better than it was. Not long ago, as we were informed by those who live close by, at least eighty cows were kept on these premises. Some of them were stowed away in a cellar in which there was scarcely a ray of light. Such things can scarcely be credited. In several of the metropolitan cowsheds, the animals are tethered so closely together that they have barely room to lie down, and in this position they are allowed to remain month after month.

Fig. 26.—Ashlin's Place, Drury Lane. A London Dairy, 1863.

The pavement of this court is in a bad state; and, knowing the condition of some of the pumps near, we looked with suspicion at one which is there. In this case, however, fortunately it is not for the purpose of drawing water from a surface well, but from a cistern under the ground, which is supplied by the ordinary water-service. Even this is not without objection, for the cistern is liable to all the pollution of the loaded atmosphere. It will be a great advantage when, instead of being forced to rely on pits of poisoned water, such neighbourhoods as this can be constantly supplied from the main.

There are other cow-sheds in the neighbourhood which should not be allowed. It is cruel to the dumb beasts and injurious to the health of human beings to keep cows in such situations.

Slowly, very slowly do knowledge and experience overcome prejudices and the apparent interest of individuals. It is the duty of all to help in this most desirable object,—not merely their duty but their interest.

Many years have passed since we first pressed on the attention of the public the fact that the extent and danger of the undercurrents of London society were not duly known and understood: that, lying in the dark shadows of London, bred in town swamps, and living in the midst of vice, ignorance, dirt, and social degradation, an army of rough and desperate men and women existed, unsuspected and uncared for. They are to be counted in thousands. An execution or a local riot sometimes brings them into daylight and the streets; but at ordinary times they are to be found only where they live massed together, and under such conditions that improvement is impossible. We have shown some of these slums, and how they act on the condition and character of the inmates; the effect on the children born in them; and the danger to all constantly resulting from the existence of such a state of things. From these vice-producing quarters the prisons are supplied, and in these places the convict, when liberated from prison, finds his base of operations in continuing what with him is viewed as the business of his life. These spots, this aggregation, are well known to the police and authorities, and it seems strange that they should be allowed to remain without some efforts at suppression and distribution.

Such haunts as these, it may be noticed, generally lie in situations which are reached through complicated turnings. Take, for instance, the neighbourhood of Lamb and Flag Court, near the Sessions House, Clerkenwell Green, where narrow courts and alleys run in all directions, like the burrows of a rabbit-warren, so that the inhabitants have the opportunity of returning to or leaving their homes in many varied directions. Costermongers and others live in parts here, but there are also many inhabitants who for years past have never earned a penny honestly. In such neighbourhoods will be found marine store-shops, the proprietors of which manage their business loosely, and in many cases are receivers of stolen goods. There are also low beer-shops, to which well-known thieves and those connected with them resort, and where *business* is arranged. The management of beer-houses calls for the attention of the Home Secretary.

The large body of people who prey upon the honest portion of the community—the ticket-of-leave men, returned convicts—chiefly live in the most wretched homes; and there is every indication that, although there may be short and sudden glimpses of prosperity, upon the whole the trade is a bad one, and that, after all, "honesty is the best policy." Even in connexion with a successful stroke of business, a chief part of the plunder goes to the receiver, and the remainder is usually rapidly spent in dissipation, waste, and drunkenness.

Many pictures might be sketched in the locality just mentioned, but we will pass on to Argyle Square, King's Cross. At the south-west corner of this square, which is formed of good houses, inhabited by respectable families, there are some narrow roadways and passages which lead towards Cromer Street and Judd Street. Various depredations have taken place around here, and but a short time ago an old gentleman was knocked down in the open street, and robbed in the forenoon and the bright sunlight. Since then a policeman has been kept on duty at this point; and the officer will tell the inquirer that there is sufficient need for his supervision, for thieves and their companions abound.

After leaving Argyle Square there may be seen an immense cow-shed, which can often be scented from afar, and cannot be healthful for those dwelling around. Nearly opposite to this is a public-house, and at the side of it are a narrow pathway and a long row of houses, many, if not all, of which are inhabited by thieves, and the women, and in some cases children, who live with them. In the morning, and until towards the afternoon, these houses are quieter than those which in other quarters are occupied by working people. Now and then, however, doubtful-looking characters may be seen skulking to and from these houses; but for the chief part the inmates are resting from their unlawful labours. The houses towards the front have a decent appearance, and of the majority the front doors are open. The writer knocked at the door of many rooms, but without receiving any response. Either the inmates had, by some telegraphic communication from house to house, been told that a strange inquirer was in the neighbourhood, or (the time was between twelve and one in the day) they were sleeping after the labours of the preceding night.

At the time above mentioned one might walk here without suspecting that anything was wrong; but as the evening approaches the dwellers come forth; and towards midnight, and late in the morning, this place is a kind of Pandemonium, the women being often more violent and drunken than the men.

In the streets leading from Drury Lane, too, there are, as our readers know well, many notorious spots. Amongst these there are, perhaps, none much worse than parts of the Coal Yard. There many thieves find harbour. Barley Court and some of the houses adjoining are almost entirely occupied by returned convicts, ticket-of-leave men, and other bad characters, both men and women. In fact, Barley Court is one of the worst places in the metropolis. No man could enter it at night with safety. Not only would he be robbed, but stripped and turned into the street. Evil women and thieves of the worst class reside there. Dr. Bennett, the medical officer of St. Giles's Workhouse, recently said it had come to his knowledge that a man had been robbed in one of the houses and stripped naked, and that the thieves had then rolled a blanket round him, stitched him up in it so that he could not move a limb, and thrust him in that condition into the street, with a large label, on which was written the word "Thief!" pinned over his breast. Surely the allowing of such dens of infamy to exist, in which the most notorious characters assemble for the worst purposes, shows either that the power of the law at present is not sufficient, or that the police are not sufficiently active in dispersing such dangerous communities.

One of our engravings (Fig. 27) represents a long court in the Coal Yard, which, like the other spots mentioned, has several entrances. The width of this court is about thirty-one inches, and in one part the wooden building very nearly touches the opposite side. Barley Court (Fig. 28) is near this, and may be reached either from Smart's Buildings, Drury Lane, or other points. We

Fig. 27.—A Narrow Alley in the Coal Yard, Drury Lane.

Fig. 28.—Barley Court. Who sowed the Tares?

last saw this locality about three in the afternoon, and found the place rather noisy. Women, muddled and tipsy, were singing ribald songs. The people crowded about were more dangerous and savage than a tribe of Caffres. In some of the rooms here, we were informed on the spot (November, 1863), three families often sleep in each.

It is very disheartening to view this class of society; to consider its extent, and the little chance there is of doing good either by punishment or persuasion; and one cannot but admit that this foul blot on the civilization of the nineteenth century has been caused by many years of neglect. Houses, unfit for the occupation of human beings, were left without care or inspection; great districts rose into existence without due provision of schools and churches; and thousands of the metropolitan population were allowed to be born in filth, and reared in ignorance, bad health, and vice. Few troubled themselves to go into those places when the monster, which has become so troublesome, had been allowed to grow to strength. We have now better agencies at work. The ragged-schools effect good, and the Homes connected with them often save those who are on the brink of crime; while the reformatories for those who are young, and have just been convicted of theft, will be the means of training many into industrious habits. A strong effort, however, is needed. The children, in such spots as those we have illustrated, if left to the course of events, can scarcely escape the moral sewer: they will be swept away to vice and crime, — misery and early death. It would be *cheaper* for society to send these children to a first-class boarding school, and put them in a way to be healthy and wise, than to allow them to become, as they probably will, thieves and prostitutes. It is not even a question between prevention and cure. Educate the children downwards to convicts, and cure is very nearly impossible. If you would do anything you must prevent.

In order to show more clearly the extent of the cost of our pauper and criminal population, we give the following figures. The population of the United Kingdom in 1861 was 29,036,508, and the number of paupers relieved in 1861 was 945,269, at a cost of £5,778,943 for England and Wales; 164,000 paupers, Ireland, at a cost of £584,348; and the number for Scotland, 97,000, at a cost of £618,000. The numbers and cost, according to these figures, would be as under:—

Paupers.		Cost.
945,269	England and Wales	£5,778,943
164,000	Ireland	584,348
97,000	Scotland	618,000
1,206,269		£6,981,291

In England and Wales, in 1861, there were committed 50,809 indictable offences: the persons apprehended numbered 27,174; persons tried, 18,326; persons convicted, 13,879; offences determined summarily, 394,717; convictions, 263,200. The charges and convictions in Ireland and Scotland bring the grand total of crimes in Great Britain to the following immense numbers; viz., crimes and offences, 479,723; convictions, 308,115.

In England and Wales—1861—there were 10,876 convicts in prison; 3,753 convicts were discharged; 1,645 convicts discharged on tickets-of-leave; 1,350 convicts discharged, expirees; 610 convicts discharged, sent to Western Australia; there were 147,971 prisoners in county and borough gaols; 130,571 prisoners discharged; 5,414 prisoners in reformatories, schools of industry, &c.; 1,298 prisoners in reformatories, schools of industry, &c., discharged; and 123,000 known depredators at large (according to the Home Office statistics).

In 1861, for the suppression of crime there was an army of 20,760 police; and the cost of the police alone, in this year, was £1,579,200; and of gaols, prisons, prosecutions, &c., £2,768,500: altogether, £4,347,700 for the suppression of crime; and this, added to the annual cost of pauperism, would give the sum of £11,327,991.

When we think of this enormous outlay for one year, only for pauperism and crime, and that as regards the latter (if we may except the operations of the industrial and reformatory schools to which the younger class of offenders are sent), little actual permanent good has been done, we look with anxiety to means for the prevention of crime which are far less expensive, and more sure in their good effect than those to which we have referred.

The good result of ragged schools and of industrial homes, which are branch establishments connected with the former, has been proved beyond a doubt, and we feel certain that a large extension of the system in the metropolis and other chief towns would save a great amount of crime. The good effect of these institutions is evident to all who will take the trouble to look into the matter. Go to those dens to which we have referred, where vice is bred, and then pass into one of the schools that, with struggles and difficulties, have been opened in the midst of poverty and degradation.

CHAPTER VIII.

THE ITALIAN QUARTER.

AMONGST those who throng the dwellings in the back parts of Drury Lane and Gray's-Inn Lane, Saffron Hill, the neighbourhood of Hockley-in-the-Hole, and some other localities in the metropolis, the wandering Italians, familiar to all who live in London, call for notice. The Italians who come in great numbers to London are of different classes, and have strayed from various parts of their beautiful country. Some of them are casters and vendors of plaster images,—others manufacture and sell barometers, or cheap picture-frames,—more travel with "shows," organs, and animals of various descriptions; while a considerable number become waiters and servants at inns. Far away from their mountain home and their friends, these strangers, in their different ways, make exertions in order to save a sum of money with which to return and purchase some little property that will enable them to supply their simple wants in inexpensive neighbourhoods.

In England, Germany, through the wild wastes of Russia, and in other countries, the Italians, real missionaries of art, spread both instruction and amusement. Before menageries were regularly established, they roamed about with dancing bears, camels, and other animals. A considerable number of these visitors come from the north of Italy: these are generally more intelligent, and are better off than the poor peasants who are natives of the Apennine region. The former of these come principally from the lakes of Upper Italy, and the valleys and declivities of the Alps. In these parts it has been the custom for many generations for the inhabitants of each district to follow some distinct branch of industry; for instance, one place sends forth vendors of barometers and mathematical and philosophical instruments; another place, stone-cutters; a third, house-painters and whitewashers; another, masons; while the manufacturers of plaster figures come chiefly from Lucca.

In some instances these workmen only travel to such a distance that they are able to return in winter, after they have completed a summer's labour. Others during the winter manufacture toys and other saleable things, and they travel in the summer and dispose of them in the adjoining states. To such an extent is the roving disposition of the portion of the Italians above referred to indulged, that it is seldom one-tenth of the male population is at home. The cultivation of the soil, which in many cases is but ill adapted to the purposes of husbandry, is generally managed by the women. At a very early age many of the boys are engaged to persons who have acquired a certain amount of capital and experience. Some of them learn the art of figure casting and painting, and others are intrusted with white mice or an organ. A stated sum is agreed to be paid for their services, the employer providing them with food, lodging, and clothing, and depending for his remuneration upon the amount of the earnings of the lads. In London and other places, where the distance will permit it, the boys return with the result of each day's work to one of the lodgings just mentioned, and there receive their humble fare. If, however, they take a wider range, they may be absent for several days, under which circumstances they would purchase their own cheap food and shelter, and would hand over the money remaining on their return.

It may be, by this arrangement, that one Italian has more than a dozen lads of different ages in his employ, some of whom, in addition to their musical instruments, have monkeys, white mice, dogs, and other animals. This arrangement leads to mischief; for the master, anxious to gain as much as he can, and, perhaps, not being aware of the danger, in a sanitary point of view, crowds the sleepers into an insufficient space, and thus causes injury to health. In some of the inconvenient houses in the neighbourhoods alluded to, several bands of Italians may be found lodged in the different apartments. Of late, the sanitary police has effected much good amongst them; for although the overcrowding is still great, attention has been shown to cleanliness.

Some of the Italians, who originally came to London in the poorest condition, have accumulated considerable sums of money. Formerly, when bears, camels, hyenas, were a fashionable exhibition, successful Italians speculated in these creatures to a considerable extent. It was not always that one poor man could afford the cost of the hire of the whole creature; so it was customary for two travellers to agree to take two quarters, the proprietor retaining two, and all the profits of the wandering were divided in the due proportions. Hand-organs are lent, to those who can be trusted, at a certain rent: these instruments have been greatly improved; and, notwithstanding that a difference of opinion exists, it is clear that much pleasure is afforded by them in places where better music cannot be heard.

So far as we have seen, both those who have charge of the young Italians and those who have the management of the lodging-houses provided for their reception are willing to attend to suggestions for improvement. It would be beneficial to institute a more rigorous examination, particularly during the night, and for the sake of these poor strangers to enforce the regulations made for the metropolitan lodging-houses.

It is asserted, on good authority, that there are in the metropolis 16,000 children trained to crime, 15,000 men living by low gambling, 50,000 by constant thieving, 5,000 receivers of stolen goods, and 150,000 men and women subsisting by other disgraceful means. There are not fewer than 25,000 beggars. So that there are more than 250,000 persons in the London district, of all ages and sexes, who prey upon the honest and industrious part of the community. These are terrible figures. It is right to say that there is a difference of opinion as to the exact amount of the evil, but none deny that it is enormous.

This is a matter, however, on which there should be no doubt. We ought to know clearly and distinctly the extent of the evil which exists, in order to be able, with proper strength, to face the danger. A searching inquiry into the condition of the metropolis is one of the necessities of the age. We want some correct data by which to judge of the increase or decrease of evil conditions: we should know to what extent the police and prisons have had the effect of checking crime: we should have evidence respecting the working of the detective body of the police force; and know if it would be advisable to increase this power or to give greater strength to the more visible part of the police.

Children have been called the poetry of the earth, beams of light, and "living jewels dropp'd unstain'd from heaven." As Longfellow writes, beautifully:—

> "Childhood is the bough where slumber'd
> Birds and blossoms many number'd."

If society get but a gnarled, deformed, and hurtful stump instead of a flowering, gladdening, good-giving tree, the blame and crime are society's own. Every child is a white page on which may be written good things; an impressible mass which waits to receive beautiful forms. The blame be on those who permit the page to be blurred, and the forms to be made repulsive. Children are the sacred trust of the State. The neglect of this trust—a great sin—brings its own great punishment.

There is danger to the State in the increase of large masses of neglected poor: and these masses are supplied from the heaps of neglected children who survive the dangers they are exposed to.

We have at various times explored some of those most forlorn refuges for the destitute, the "casual wards" of the metropolitan workhouses, and certainly never saw anything more disgraceful to a great and civilized city than is the state of most of them. A few years since, in some of these dens, not even a low wooden partition was provided to separate one unfortunate lodger from another. The sexes were separated; but in other respects nothing could be worse than the arrangement of the accommodation provided by many parishes for the destitute poor. We have in our mind fearful pictures of men, women, and children lying at the workhouse doors at midnight, in inclement weather; and remember when, having passed this human barrier, by the help of the "bull's eye" of the watchman, we have with difficulty waded through the sleeping bodies of destitute persons who occupied the whole of the long passage, the heads and shoulders raised against one wall, and the knees and feet pressed against the other. On opening the door leading to some of these dormitories, the poisonous atmosphere was almost sufficient to suffocate a stranger, and prevent him from seeing the close pack of human beings collected there: not even straw was provided. Until the light of the watchman was thrown into the place, it was in total darkness; some of the men were quite naked, having made a pillow of their ragged clothes. Few who have not seen these "wards" would believe that such things could be in our own day in this Christian land; and yet these poor persons were thankful for the shameful shelter, and perhaps thought with pity of those who were lying at the workhouse-gate.

We will not distress our readers by further picturing the appearance of some of these casual wards, in which human beings are huddled together in the most disgraceful manner. The story has been already told. Some improvement has been lately made, and we hope that more will be speedily effected. It is a difficult question, we know. We have no wish to make pauperism pleasant, but men and women must not be allowed to perish of cold and hunger in the streets.

CHAPTER IX.

THE CITY ROAD : NEEDLE-WOMEN.

IT would need a long life, completely devoted, to acquire more than a very superficial knowledge of the varied features of this vast metropolis. Look at the labyrinth of streets, roads, and lanes, filled with a dense population, getting their living somehow, going on continuously in poverty from youth to manhood, and from manhood to the grave; and consider how little of all this is known to the generality of those who form the richer part of the remarkable whole. Many of the districts have a character of their own, and all give matter for thought to reflective wanderers. The spot to which accident has led us in the City Road, a triangle bounded by that great thoroughfare, by East Road, Murray Street, and Edward Street, leading up to Wharf Road, including the Eagle Tavern, is but a small patch, but it is covered with buildings, densely inhabited, and shows a peculiar style of dwelling, which, in consequence of decay and the awakened spirit of improvement, is fast disappearing. The City Road, although lined with buildings that are irregular and without beauty, is picturesque and striking. Trees are struggling in the front gardens of public houses, while in what were the fore-courts of other residences, are shed-like shops, occupied by photographers, pigeon-dealers, bird-cage makers, and the pursuers of other unsettled occupations.

Walking along Mount Row—a short cut, which in the morning and evening is thronged with well-dressed wayfarers, proceeding to and from business—we come to Winckworth Buildings, on which is the date 1766, a time when many of the dwellings here were built. Long streets of small two-story houses pass in various directions, some in irregular lines; others, of a more modern build, are on a regular plan, the streets running at right angles; and it is worthy of remark, and very fortunate, that the chief thoroughfares are wide and of great length. There are, however, some narrow passages, in which the usual corresponding amount of sickness is to be met with.

It is understood that the neighbourhood is generally well drained and tolerably healthy. This may partly be attributed to the gravelly soil. Moneyer Street, Union Street, Cross Street, and some other parts must, however, be excepted, and further steps should be taken to get rid of the cesspools which are there to be met with. Most of the rooms in the houses are very small, and many of them overcrowded with families. Here the usual complaint is made of the want of cleanliness and sanitary knowledge. One visitor, who is much engaged amongst the poor, speaks of the difficulty there is in getting them to attend to matters which may save life and health. Some think themselves insulted if suggestions be made to them. As an instance of the need there is for diffusing knowledge of the means by which life may be preserved, it may be mentioned that a decent-looking woman lately hurried to a surgeon in this neighbourhood, and stated that her female child was in convulsions. He gave her some medicine, and told her to put the child into a hot bath. Some hours afterwards she came back to say that the child was still in fits. On this the surgeon, surprised, went to see what was the matter, and found her standing in a pail, naked, in the draught of two doors, with her feet in about three inches of water! Such an occurrence, and a hundred others that might be mentioned, show, as we have often urged, the great need that exists for making the general laws of health a part of education in our national and other schools. It is difficult to deal with the adults of the present generation, but we may work usefully on those who are rising. The Ragged Schools and Reformatories, we repeat, are proving their usefulness. These are checking juvenile crime, which, in a large majority of cases, is the result of the want of right employment, or the chance of doing well. Reared in poverty, accustomed from the earliest years to neglect and the worst kinds of vice, thousands have been made into dangerous and expensive criminals, with little will of their own. In a marked way Ragged Schools are improving the children in some of the worst parts of the metropolis. These schools, in which earnest men and women devotedly labour, are hidden in back slums from the view of the more prosperous classes of the community. It is most important, however, that they should be visited, and that all should in their various ways assist in supporting them and extending their usefulness.

The cost of crime in Great Britain, and of its evil results, is enormous. The statistics which prove that since the introduction of these schools and reformatories, the convictions for illegal offences amongst the young have declined at the rate of from 25 to 30 per cent., ought to obtain for them increased aid. It has been shown that the teaching of these institutions is more useful than that of the prison, the hulks, or the hangman.

In some parts around, the houses have a squalid appearance: none more so than Mount Pleasant. Northward; beyond Murray Street, houses of a better and larger description have sprung up, which gain by the contrast. The vast assemblages of streets and squares of houses of a good class which stretch quite to Kingsland, and almost to Dalston and Newington, have grown up like mushrooms. Little more than twenty years ago Murray Street abutted upon the fields. Since then London has stretched upwards of two miles in that direction. The increase of the population of Hoxton and the adjoining districts has been immense.

In a shop not far from Nile Street, which was literally filled with stalls and "Buy, buy, buyers," a number of poor women were waiting, probably to be paid. It is said that there are in the metropolis more than 30,000 women who earn a miserable income by the various departments of needlework.

The large users of needlework, the makers of soldiers' and other rough clothing, in many instances carry out a system which is constantly pressing upon the very poorest. They give out their work to a certain limited number of persons who are able to find security for the materials. These persons are every now and then underworking each other. Having undertaken a particular amount of work, to be completed in a given time, and at the lowest cost, these sub-contractors look around for assistance, and perhaps each distributes the materials to seven, eight, or more persons, who are in a less prosperous condition than themselves, but who are "good" for the value entrusted to them. These again often divide the work. Each process must, of course, be attended with profit, and so does this system work that the sum which comes to the actual sewer, the poorest of the whole, is not sufficient to procure the commonest necessaries of life.

In Whitechapel and other eastern districts women may be met with who have been well brought up and in comfortable circumstances, and who, by incessant labour for sixteen or seventeen hours a day, can with difficulty earn in the week 3s. 6d. Even this miserable remuneration is declining, and there is a difficulty in getting regular work. This, in some measure, may be attributed to the use of the sewing-machine, not only in the houses of the rich and middle classes, but also of the large manufacturing clothiers, and amongst the sub-contractors to whom we have referred.

Terrible sufferings, temptations, and troubles beset those who have no reliance but on this kind of work. Such is their hopeless condition, that we cannot help whispering a belief that, though the immediate distress might be much, it would be an advantage if the needle and thread were altogether superseded, and placed in the Brompton Museum with the flint-and-steel tinder-box, the spinning-wheel, and other curiosities.

During the past few years, praiseworthy efforts have been made to better the condition of needle-women; and we believe that, in a few large and important millinery establishments in the fashionable quarters, improved arrangements prevail. Homes have been opened for the use of young women engaged at those places; and lately an institution has been established in Lamb's Conduit Street, for the same class. It is a matter of surprise and sorrow to notice how slowly such means as these are appreciated by the classes whom they are intended to serve. The proper development of women is one of the most urgent and important social problems of the time. The question needs to be looked at, not from a prejudiced or an old-world point of view, but with thoughts of the changed conditions of society, and the marvellous discoveries and improvements which have been made. The electric telegraph is weekly extending employment to educated and respectable females. The increase of national schools, not only in this country, but in the colonies, opens out a source of income to those who are fitted to instruct. When we have met in dismal dens women of superior ability in great poverty, we have thought of the need there is for intelligent nurses for the sick, and that they might thus usefully employ themselves. In houses of the middle classes it is particularly desirable that "Mrs. Gamp" should be superseded by women of a different stamp; and much good would be done if arrangements could be made on an extensive scale, so that females might undergo an examination as to their fitness for nursing, not only the sick, but young children. Females with diplomas of ability in this respect and certificates of character would be much sought after and well paid. Removing the pressure from other kinds of employment would improve the condition of those remaining in them.

Poor woman! poor woman! And yet, as our greatest female poet says—

> "Be satisfied.
> Something thou hast to bear through womanhood—
> Peculiar suffering answering to the sin,
> Some pang laid down for each new human life;
> Some weariness in guarding such a life,
> Some coldness from the guarded. But thy love
> Shall chant its own beatitudes
> After its own life working. A child's kiss
> Set on thy sighing lips shall make thee glad;
> A poor man served by thee shall make thee rich;
> A sick man helped by thee shall make thee strong."

Our triangle of houses has more than three sides, and offers many points of view, but we may not look farther.

CHAPTER X.

OLD LONDON.

WE come at beliefs by a gradual process; first theoretically, then experimentally; then by confirmatory proof: thus ascertained, they pass for granted; and the young learn them by rote, as matters of course. In this way early information or knowledge must be always looked upon as curious, —as a link in the development of civilization. To trace the opinions of our ancestors through successive ages is like watching a blind man groping along a road. Now we think he will find the clue; now we see he has missed it, and must grope and grope again before he comes within reach of it once more; so in the gradual accumulation of the codes necessary to civilization, here and there a law points to an advance almost beyond the requirements of the time, and which subsequent ages have lost sight of in their daily practice, and they have had to bear the consequences in disastrous blunders. For instance, a sanitary decree was issued by that wise sovereign lady, Elizabeth, when she enacted that "No owner or occupier of any cottage shall place or willingly suffer any more families than one to cohabit therein: in pain to forfeit to the lord of the leet 10s. for every month he so continues them together." In this clause we have the question of the evil of overcrowding fearlessly grasped, calculated upon, and provided against by penalties; and yet to this very day we go crowding cottages together, and crowding families in cottages. Queen Elizabeth was a wise princess, and perhaps recognized the importance of sanitary science; but instead of availing ourselves of her legislation, we prefer to go on blundering with our fevers, choleras, and other plagues, to learn for ourselves. She also made a great point of the cleansing and scouring of ditches, and the keeping of the hedges and trees in order along the highways, and in one of her regulations entering upon these matters we may see an anticipatory injunction against the modern practice of collecting scavenage in heaps and letting it lie and rot, sometimes in the centre and sometimes in the suburbs of towns:

"None shall cast the scouring of his ditch into the highway and suffer it to lie there six months: in pain to forfeit 10d. for every load."

Still earlier precaution for the preservation of the public health was taken by Edward II., when he enacted that a butcher should not sell swine's flesh "mezzeled," or dead of the murrain. For the first offence in this particular the butcher was to be "amercied;" for the second, to have the pillory; for the third, to be imprisoned and fined; for the fourth, to abjure the town. Henry VII. took up this same sanitary scent when he decreed that "No butcher shall kill any flesh in his scalding-house, or within the walls of London: in pain to forfeit for every ox so killed 12d., and for every other beast 8d., to be divided between the king and the prosecutor." And more especially when he provided that this law was to extend to all other walled towns, Cambridge, Berwick, and Carlisle only excepted. For all this legislative wisdom, the slaughtering of cattle is with but few exceptions carried on, with apparent preference, in the narrowest alleys in the most crowded and central portions of the town. Looking over the early statutes we can see most significant proof of a perception of the vital importance of sanitary measures. Many regulations were instituted which represent a wise intelligence on the part of those who framed them. It would have been well if men in the intervening periods had not lost sight of these, and left to the present age the gigantic task of combating with the causes of preventible deaths. It is not gainsaid but that some skirmishes have already been fought on this issue; but these are not to be compared to the grand battle which has yet to be waged.

Henry VI. decreed that, in a given ten years, several persons should be sent as commissioners of sewers into all parts of the realm, to inquire into the state of the "walls, ditches, banks, gutters, sewers, gotes, calcies, bridges, streams, and other defences by the coasts of the sea and marsh ground," and to cause any of them that required to be so, to be "corrected, repaired, and amended." Henry VIII. extended this commission over an additional twenty years, and desired that the commissioners should take oath that they would execute the laws and ordinances according to their "cunning, wit, and power, without favour, meed, dread, malice, or affection." Edward VI. rendered the commission permanent.

Great attention was paid to the matter of paving in the time of Henry VIII. Every person owning tenements on the highway between Strand Cross and Charing Cross; in Holborn, between the bridge and the bars; in Southwark; in Whitechapel, from Aldgate to the church; Chancery Lane, westwards from Holborn Bars towards St. Giles's; Gray's Inn Lane; Show Lane (Shoe Lane); and Fewter Lane (Fetter Lane), was required to maintain the pavements under penalty of forfeiting 6d. for every square yard neglected. If the inhabitants of the houses paved the footways before them, they were empowered to deduct the amount from their rents. Another statute was passed by the same monarch for the paving of "Whitecross Street, Chiswell Street, Golding Lane, Grub Street, Goswell Street, Long Lane, Saint John Street, the streets then leading from the bars to Cow Cross, Water Lane in Fleet Street, the streets behind St. Clement's Church without Temple Bar; the way from the west bars in Tothill Street, in Westminster, to the west end of Petit France; the way without Bishopsgate above Shoreditch Church; Strand Bridge, and the way leading thence towards Temple Bar; and Foscoe Lane, leading down to Strand Bridge." Thus we can trace the gradual paving of London, and the gradual incorporation of suburb after suburb. Elizabeth continues the useful work, passing an Act for paving and keeping in repair "the way with Algate called the Bars with Algate; another leading from the old cage there to the north end of Nightingale Lane; and another between the said old cage and Crossmill, in the parish of St. Mary;" and instituted a fine of 3s. 4d. for every square yard not so paved and repaired; and also provided for the "scouring and cleansing of certain ditches thereabouts;" and subsequently to this another Act for the paving of the Minories and the cleansing of the ditch in Hog Lane, which last sanitary measure was to be carried out at the cost of the owners of the lands lying on the north side of the said lane, under a penalty of 6s. 8d. for every pole left "unscoured." In the reign of her successor, St. Giles-in-the-Fields and Drury Lane were paved according to Act of Parliament.

Throughout the masses, however, the greatest ignorance of sanitary science prevailed, and plagues devastated the land. By one outbreak, in the 14th century, so great was the destruction of human life throughout the whole land that grass grew in the streets of the once populous cities, the price of provisions and animals of labour decreased, in consequence of the want of buyers, to a remarkable extent; and, in some places, the living were not sufficient to bury the dead.

From all the accounts which can now be gathered, this visitation was general throughout the whole population. There were then few towns much better situated as regards sanitary arrangements than that which has become so great a metropolis. Worse drained and even worse supplied with pure water than in the days of the Roman occupation, the impurities of the soil increased, the houses were closely built together within the walls of the cities, the offal of the slaughter-houses and other refuse were carelessly allowed to accumulate, the dead filling the graveyards, and personal cleanliness was not so carefully attended to as it was even by the Saxon. There is reason to believe that one-fourth of the population of London was carried off by an outbreak of the plague in the 14th century. The result of after-attacks was equally frightful, but need not be dwelt on.

With the exception of Winchester Street, in the City, there is not now remaining in the metropolis any street which enables us so well to form an idea of old London as those represented in the accompanying engravings, and before long these, too, will be demolished. The bill lately submitted to Parliament for clearing this district of its houses was thrown out, but the attempt will probably not end there, and the whole of the houses lying between the Strand and Wych Street will doubtless soon be pulled down. Much as we may admire the picturesque and value old structures,—landmarks in our history,— we can express no sorrow in this case. One of the views here given (Fig. 29) represents Wych Street, looking towards the east. Another (Fig. 30) shows Holywell Street, of evil notoriety, looking in the same direction. We have already illustrated and described some ancient parts of Drury Lane. In the Coal Yard, at the Holborn end of Drury Lane, Nell Gwynne was born. Adjoining the Cock and Pie Fields was a considerable extent of land, called the Aldewych Close and Aldewych Fields. From these Wych Street takes its name. The title seems to show that in the Saxon times a suburban village, or wych, stood here, which in succeeding ages had passed away. In an old map dating about 1300, these fields are shown, and the present course of Drury Lane is marked *Via de Aldewych*.

In 1662, William d'Avenant, on quitting the cockpit, built the Duke's Theatre, on a portion of the Aldewych field, and a part became the property of Sir Henry Drury, in the reign of Queen Elizabeth. On this point Pennant says, " Drury Lane, the modern of the Aldewych Road, originated from Drury House, which was built, I believe, by Sir William Drury, a most able commander in the Irish wars, who unfortunately fell in a duel with Sir John Burroughs, in a foolish quarrel about precedence. Sir Robert Drury, his son, was a great patron of Dr. Donne, and assigned him apartments within this house." This mansion stood near the bottom of the lane, on the south of Aldewych Close,

Fig. 29.—Wych Street, Strand; as seen looking towards the East.

and in St. Clement's parish. On its site William Lord Craven, created earl in 1673, built a magnificent residence. It seems that this mansion was allowed to fall into decay, and was afterwards a place of public entertainment, known by the sign of the Queen of Bohemia. Craven Buildings now stand on the site of this house.

Some idea of the respectability at one time of part of Drury Lane may be formed from the following list of inhabitants in 1623:—Sir John Cotton, Sir Thomas Finch, the Earl of March, Sir Francis Kynasten, Sir Lewis Lewknor, Sir Edmund Lenthall, Sir Edward Peto, Sir Antony Bugg, Sir Antony Henton, Philip Parker, esquire, Sir Gilbert Houghton, Lady

Fig. 30.—Holywell Street; looking towards the East.

Henage, Sir Lewis Tresham, Sir John Sydnam, Lady Lambert, and others.

In the old map above mentioned, at the bottom of the Via de Aldewych, two lanes take the course of the present streets, one leading to Holywell Street, and the other continuing straight down to the Strand, opposite Somerset House. This is called Maypole Lane, and shows that, in times now remote, the Maypole was raised in merry May time, in the Strand, near the spot now occupied by the recently-erected drinking-fountain. Holywell Street had its name from a well of reputation, said to be under the Old Dog tavern, and supplying, it is asserted, the Roman Bath opposite the end of Newcastle Street, in the Strand. This, however, is getting out of our course.

CHAPTER XI.

OUR HOUSES AND OUR HEALTH.

WE cannot yet abandon generalities, although it is time we should be able to do so. The public are not yet even sufficiently awake to the importance of the matter to enable us to give up general observations in order to clear the way, and induce a strong current of public opinion to lead to change in the right direction. Further evidence of the connexion between evil structural arrangements and disease ought not to be necessary, but unfortunately it is. When we find in one parish—St. Pancras, for example—that in one district (Cavendish) the average number of deaths per annum is 15 in 1,000, while in another (Christ Church) 23 die in 1,000; that in St. James's parish, in one division (St. James's), 12 die in 1,000, while in another (Berwick Street) 28 die each year in 1,000; and that certain dwellings furnish a regular supply of fever cases, which supply stops when structural improvements are made, doubts on the subject should surely vanish. It may be affirmed that there are thousands of houses where health, decency, or virtue is scarcely possible. The devotion of some years to the subject, at the risk, perhaps, on more than one occasion, of life, must be our justification for thinking and speaking strongly on the matter. It is scarcely necessary to multiply proofs of the advantages that follow improved dwellings; but the decrease of mortality in model lodging-houses, published some time ago, should not be passed by. The effect of construction and overcrowding has, again, been remarkably shown in barracks and hospitals. At Scutari, where at one time there were 2,500 inmates, two out of five died, or 40 per cent. In hospital tents in the Crimea, without shelter, food, or medicine, not more than half that mortality occurred; and in huts well placed and arranged, the mortality of wounded was only three per cent. Gangrene and erysipelas haunt some hospitals, and are not to be found in others. The startling effect produced by the announcement of the death-rate in the army at home will be remembered. The cause was evident when the barracks were examined, and the mortality has been lessened immensely by compliance with sanitary requirements. We have the deposition of medical officers of health, that, in streets which had been distinguished by sickness, the improvement of the sewers and the proper drainage of the houses have been followed by diminished sickness. The probable sites of epidemics can be pointed out; unhealthy districts are obvious.

A strong public opinion is fortunately growing up on the subject, and one result will doubtless be the improvement of the houses, not only of the labouring population, but of all classes. An assertion which we ventured to make some years ago, "*As the home, so the people*," is beginning to fix itself in the popular mind. We find it, with humble satisfaction, the text of essays and the motto of associations. Widely admitted, it would be certain to produce good fruit. We would add to this another:—

> To drain and pave,
> Means raise and save.

The connexion, perhaps, is not at once obvious, but it is, nevertheless, undeniable. Drainage alone will not do everything, but it is an important first step. Returns from Salisbury, for example, show that the average number of deaths annually, in 1,000, before drainage, was nearly 28, and after drainage, not 21. In Ely, the deaths in 1,000 were, before drainage, 25¾, and since the drainage, but 20¾. The efforts that have been made have had their effect in ridding many evil localities of fever; and recently it has been noticed that the same fever has haunted houses of a higher grade,—a fever which physicians have shown is caused by the emanations of decomposing matter,—the foul air, for example, of drains and cesspools. Of the evils of cesspools it is impossible to speak too strongly. The condition of London in this respect, at one time, was frightful. If the surface could have been taken off, we should have seen a bubbling expanse of putridity and filth horrible to behold. Dante's rain brought scarcely greater horrors,—

> "Stank all the world whereon that tempest fell."

Five thousand cesspools have been got rid of (says Dr. Letheby) in the City alone.

And now let us look to some of the structural defects to be found in our dwelling-houses. Prominently, we may enumerate bad foundation,—permitting dampness; thin and porous walls,—contributing to the same evil, and increasing the cost of firing; defective drains and traps; want of ventilation—supply of pure air and removal of bad; insufficient height of rooms; want of pure water; wasteful means of heating; smoky chimneys; want of light,—the legacy of the old window-tax (dark rooms give a larger amount of sickness than light ones); the defective paving of yards and areas; and the excessive cost of houses for the poorer classes.

We would refer briefly to a few inventions and materials bearing on some of these heads, not necessarily the best of their kind, but those that are accessible, and which will serve to hang observations on. In respect of dampness, one of the latest inventions counteracting it in foundations is Taylor's damp-proof course, an elongation in vitrified earth of the ordinary air-brick, and which, while keeping damp down, lets in sufficient air to the joists of the lower floors to make them dry, and prevent them from rotting. Mr. George Jennings's burnt-earth air-bricks are similar to the iron air-brick, but larger and more ornamental, and deserve to be used. The provision of a couple of common iron air-bricks for the ventilation of the whole basement of a house, as used by house-builders (the current often stopped by the joists), is altogether insufficient for the purpose. In many cases there should be a layer of concrete over the whole site of a building to keep down emanations; sometimes even of asphalte. Pipe drainage for the surface is often advisable. Hollow walls are drier and warmer than solid walls of the same cost. Some difficulty has been found in tying together the two sides of a hollow wall, and Mr. Jennings makes a bond brick for the purpose, which promises to be useful. We have had some experience of hollow walls, and have reason to think them advantageous. There are various facing bricks which deserve notice. And as to the question of using absorbent or non-absorbent bricks for the walls of houses, they should at any rate be non-absorbent externally. Internally, for cottages, a non-absorbent (and heat-conducting) material has been objected to; for hospitals, however, it would seem necessary to use it. The Poole Architectural Pottery Company make bricks coloured and glazed externally, which deserve attention. Many specimens of improved bricks, as well as other building materials, may be seen in the South Kensington Museum; and many experiments have been tried there with new cements and modes of building, the statement of which would be valuable. The injurious effects of damp in cottages and other dwellings are not sufficiently appreciated. We must all know rooms, such as we have already pointed to, where the paper peels off, where a book becomes mouldy, linen wet, and which are, nevertheless, constantly inhabited by reasoning and instructed beings, who expect to enjoy health. And how can there be other than such rooms? See the mode in which thousands of houses in the suburbs of the metropolis and elsewhere are commenced: without any excavation; the basement floor of thin gaping boards placed within six inches of the damp ground; with slight walls of ill-burnt bricks and muddy mortar, sucking up the moisture and giving it out in the apartments; ill-made drains, untrapped, pouring forth bad air; and you scarcely need more causes, although others exist, for a low state of health. In the case of thousands of houses built at present in the metropolis, no architect is ever employed. The public should know this, that the opprobrium to be incurred by such buildings may not be cast upon architects. We are much disposed to think that the Legislature should further interfere, and that some properly constituted officer should certify that every new house is built in such a manner as to be fit to live in. Let us hope, at all events, that the Metropolitan Building Act will be amended. The only three provisions in the Building Act framed for the preservation of the public health—those relating to cellar-dwellings, rooms in the roof, and an area of 100 feet behind each house not wholly lighted from the street—are in practice inoperative. With regard to rooms in the roof, they are made with a door and a place for light; they are formed sufficiently large to allow of a bedstead being put up; but if the district surveyor summon the builder for making them of less height than is required by the Act, the latter has simply to testify that they are not sleeping-rooms at all, but places for luggage, and the result is, that the district surveyor loses his time in addition to the cost of the summons. Then, with respect to cellar-dwellings, the Act only provides that the surveyor shall be allowed to inspect such places between nine o'clock in the morning and six o'clock in the evening; which is, of course, not the time to obtain evidence to determine that they have been used as sleeping-places on the previous night. The duty of inspection, we repeat, should be thrown upon the inspector of nuisances or the police, the district surveyor simply certifying as to the structural deficiency.

The evil that results from the insufficient *trapping of drains* is immense, and widely spread. The common bell-trap is useless: the loose grating is soon broken or lost. We had occasion recently officially to examine a street of fourteen decent-looking houses in a suburb, and found that the bell-traps of nearly the whole number had disappeared. A stream of foul air was rising in each; but the people there said that there was no smell; at all events, that they could not smell anything. Their own faces and sickly children testified to the existence of that and other evil arrangements. The want of recognition is striking. We remember the case of an old woman at the back of Bishopsgate Street, who lived in a house just opposite a gully-hole, and who, when questioned as to the smell, replied: "No, sir, there isn't no smell; there has been a deal of sickness about, and I have lost my son, but I am *manured* to it, and don't mind it." There are several traps now before the public which might be adopted. That of Messrs. Tye and Andrews, for instance, for sinks, is far superior to the trap in common use; the grate is fixed, and the trap is formed with a larger quantity of water. Mr. Lovegrove has invented one which goes farther, by the application of back-flaps (or valves) to the outlets of all the various forms of hydraulic traps; so that variations of temperature which defeat traps sealed with water alone, have no effect on it. We do not mention these inventions with the desire of extolling any particular one and disparaging others; all we say is, that we want a perfect trap. Those which we now have in daily use are merely disguises, and permit a constant stream of poisonous exhalation to penetrate the house. The great thing which we have to do in directing attention to this subject is, to get the public to understand the evil; that there is something better than that which they now use, and that the sooner they get it the better. With improved traps and impermeable drain-pipes, we then call for the proper ventilation of drains outside the house. The use of the rain-water pipes for that purpose cannot always be recommended. Charcoal appears to offer the means cheaply and safely.

This brings us to the want of ventilation in our houses. All ought to insist on means being provided *to admit fresh air involuntarily*, and without draught, in every room, and *to take away foul air*. Nature arranges for vitiated air at once to sail away from us. We arrange to defeat Nature, and as in all other such cases, suffer. There are various systems on the broad principle of letting in fresh air to the fire-brick back of the stove, and so bringing it warmed into the room, and of providing an opening into a tube to take away the vitiated air. But none is used to any extent. The grates used in many houses are wasteful in the extreme. It is time some means of testing were established. The sanitary committee appointed in connexion with the last Great Exhibition had hoped to make an arrangement for the testing of grates and ranges submitted for exhibition, but were not able to bring it to bear. The open fireplace is the focus of enjoyment, and we cannot get rid of it, but we may take care that it does its work well. While some ranges cook the soldier's dinner with two and a half ounces of fuel, another burns up in the same process as many pounds. The supply of fresh air in our rooms, of which we have just spoken, would often prevent the annoyance of a smoky chimney. As to water, our present supply is most unsatisfactory. The upper Thames water is fouled by sewage, and the whole question wants discussion. The influence of impure water in producing disease is unquestionable. The cost of obtaining water pure should not be considered. The Romans were wiser than we are. As to the surface wells in towns, they are mostly poisonous. Improvement is needed in the conveyance, too, of water to our houses. Lead pipes are dangerous. This is constantly said; but we go on using them. Take the Report of the Manchester and Salford Sanitary Association. This shows conclusively that water which has remained even a few hours in lead pipes should never be used for dietary purposes. "When water remains stagnant in the pipes, it not only becomes highly charged with the dangerous poison, but a coating is formed on the inner surface of the pipes, which coating is subsequently detached by the water passing through, and which it impregnates with lead. The practice of lining lead pipes with tin affords little, and only temporary, protection, and is of no practical value. Bearing in mind that lead is a cumulative poison, that water containing it may be used for a considerable time, and the foundation be laid for great suffering and physical injury before the symptoms become so marked as to justify a medical man in pronouncing the case to be one of lead-poisoning, the discovery and adoption of pipes for domestic supply which could not be productive of this evil is of the greatest moment, especially to our densely populated labour districts. The first step towards remedying the evil is a thorough conviction of its existence, and of the serious results which may follow from disregarding its importance." Let the community at large be convinced on these points, and it is more than probable an efficient remedy would be discovered, more especially if corporations would offer to parties engaged in the necessary pursuits some inducement to produce a pipe economical in cost, easy of application, and on which the water would not act prejudicially.

Cost in all these matters is a most important element; in none more so than in constructing houses for the labouring classes. Something could be done to cheapen this by using machinery, as we have already suggested, and producing doors, windows, floors, skirtings, roofs, and so on, to suit particular plans. Of course, one would not wish the uniformity this would produce carried farther; but for the poorer classes fit and healthful accommodation at low cost is a matter of life and death. The use of concrete for cottage building has not been sufficiently tried. As to the question of agglomerated houses, so to speak, it is too large to be touched upon now. One observation, however, we must repeat, which is, that the sooner the notion is exploded that in England every one occupies a house of his own the better. Every house is built as if for one family, and then, in a large proportion of cases, comes to be occupied by several, who dwell, consequently, without comfort or conveniences. The fact that houses are to be occupied by more than one family must be looked in the face, and proper provision must be prepared, legislation being made to aid, and not to thwart this, as is now the case.

It is often forgotten that although death is attributed to some named disease, in numerous cases death would not have resulted but for the impaired or low state of health of the patient. Evil sanitary arrangements lead to this low state of health, and so to the death. It is not too much to assert that a low state of health is the chronic condition of thousands. The laws of health should be taught to every child, from the ragged-school upwards, and followed; and if we had preventive physicians

— physicians who would keep us from getting ill, as well as cure us when we are ill — we should be a healthier, better, and happier people. The spread of knowledge on the subject is of the greatest importance; to that we must look for the desired result. It is scarcely possible to estimate the amount of misery, remorse, and crime produced by unhealthy houses. Apart, however, from the avoidance of extreme evils—illness and death—a home should be a place of repose, cheerfulness, and comfort; where the worker, the bread-winner, may gain fresh strength and energy for the daily struggle. Dulness, gloom, apathy, ill-temper will not produce this. We all know what trifling matters will change a career; and that the misery of a life may be born of a chance observation. The connexion of these remarks with our subject will be seen at once. Amidst bad domestic influences the spirits flag, the temper changes. Breathing bad air, suffering from the effect of damp, the world looks dark, the heart is heavy; cheerful effort is out of the question; kindly companionship is withered; and jangle and snarl take the place of mutual encouragement and healthful converse, which develop the affections and powers. The occupants of such houses as we are contemplating do not *live;* they only pass their time—and a very bad time it not seldom is. Life, which should be a blessing, is often made a curse by an unhealthy house and its consequence—an ill-ordered home. Besides remedies of evils referred to, we want also more colour in our houses, more pictures or prints, flowers, and a garden,—the effect of these on the spirits, and so on the health, the thoughts, and the habits, is greater than some imagine; and the same argument will apply in calling for the well-ordering and proper adornment of towns.

CHAPTER XII.

EVILS IN CELLARS, SHOPS, AND YARDS.

WE must again go into details. For the preservation of the health of the dwellers in houses the proper care of the basement is of much consequence. Notwithstanding the legal provision which has been made to the contrary, thousands of families live, if it may be so called, in underground rooms in various parts of the metropolis, as we have shown, and there is in these under-parts of houses sufficient to account for much disease. In many instances, there is no other place except the cellar for the reception of the dust and other refuse, which are often allowed to remain for many weeks before they are removed. In these subterranean apartments, too, cesspools or badly appointed water-closets are often to be found. Other cellars, both in town and country, are used for the stowage of various articles: these also require improvement, particularly those in which beer is kept. With the greatest care, even in those instances where publicans deal entirely with the large brewers, it is difficult to keep the air of these receptacles pure: there is always a certain amount of waste which gets spilled, and, together with other matters, gives the air a sour and unhealthy taint. Many cellars are deeper than the neighbouring drain. In some instances the drain is broken and the sewage leaks into the place; there are often other means of pollution, which filter through the walls of the cellar. Many cellars are without flagging or any other pavement; but, if even this were attended to, when the level is below the drain, purification by washing cannot easily be managed. Moreover, in nine cases out of ten there is an entire neglect of any kind of ventilation. The sketch we give from a cellar in London (Fig. 31) represents the condition of many, where drainage matter percolates and poisons the air.

In many places throughout the country it is still the custom for each publican to brew the ale which he sells; and this requires a large amount of care; for after the partial fermentation in the brewhouse is effected, it has to be completed in the cellars. We have visited such places when the atmosphere has been almost unbearable. In some, in which large stores of ale are kept to mellow with age, small pits may be seen dug for the reception of the foul half-liquid matter that finds its way into the place. "It is the winter time, you see," says "mine host,"—"and we are afraid of a chill;" and in consequence, the smallest crevice by which air could enter is closed with straw. Sometimes, in the parts where the fermentation is carried on, charcoal and coke fires are lighted; and this, under

Fig. 31.—A Beer-cellar in London. "Taking a Drain."

the circumstances, does not cause improvement. It may be good for the ale, but it is bad for human beings. It is difficult, however, to lead those who are engaged in the business to see the matter rightly, or to agree in this opinion; and the same perversity is to be found in all ranks. We have heard a church dignitary advocate the wholesomeness of an overcrowded burial-vault beneath his church, and declare that he "would not mind sleeping in it." We have heard parish churchwardens and guardians declare that the water which was in wells into which the contents of cesspools and other filth flowed was pure and wholesome; that graveyards loaded with the dead up to within a few inches of the surface could hurt no one of the living who were crowded in the dwellings around. In like manner the owners of huge dust-heaps, horse-slaughterers, tallow-melters, and a host of other health-damagers, maintain the salubrity and pleasantness of their trade arrangements, and deny that any alteration is possible or desirable. So, too, notwithstanding the strong case which was made against the unhealthy state of the bakehouses in the metropolis, there were bakers who argued that the outcry was all nonsense, and resisted improvement.

Still, if prejudices are hard to remove, and sanitary reforms difficult to accomplish, something has been done in the bakehouse; and when once the change is made, there are none who are better satisfied than those who have been forced into it.

We will venture to predict the same in connexion with the cellars of publicans, to which, after this digression, we will return, and note that in most instances they are not arched—not even ceiled. It will be found that frequently these cellars stretch below the parlours, in which a large number of people, who live around, assemble in the evenings. The parlours are often very badly ventilated; and this circumstance, with what passes from the place below, cannot fail to cause injurious effects. Moreover, all the air in the house is impregnated with the gases that arise from the cellars; and this is most perceptible in the mornings after doors and windows have been closed.

All cellars should be carefully flagged and properly drained: there should be water-supply for cleaning, and trapped sinks in convenient situations. In the summer time, good rather than harm would be done by the free admission of air; and, where there are no means of thorough ventilation through the walls, shafts should be made which would communicate with the chimneys or the outward space. The air of the cellars should be diverted, as much as possible, from the occupied part of the house; and for this purpose arching would be of advantage; and it should be borne in mind that substantial brickwork is in itself a means of insuring the equal temperature of cellars to a considerable extent. Every householder should make a point of at once examining the condition of the basement of his residence. If this were largely done, many would be horrified. In large and even important houses, the basements and cellars are full of danger.

Looking higher up, many shops are so constructed as to add to the evils which are likely to arise from the neglected state of the cellars.

In some situations, such as the narrow and crooked streets near St. Paul's Cathedral, particularly on the south side, the carrying out of proper sanitary arrangements is a matter of difficulty; but in all cases much good is to be done by making the necessity for alterations clear. In these parts there are chandlers' shops, for example, in which candles, bacon, cheese, soap, butter, red herrings, and a hundred other miscellaneous articles, are thickly stored. In most instances, although the fronts may have been improved and modernized, the interiors are unchanged. Generally, the ceilings are low, and the shop extends as far as the space will allow, until it abuts on the adjoining premises. What has been originally a small back-yard has been built over. In some cases a skylight has been provided; in others not; but often where there is a light, it is made so that it cannot be opened, —to prevent the visits of thieves. Even when the skylight is formed to act as a ventilator, it is not used.

An examination of a number of these premises shows that, originally,— say at the time of the rebuilding after the Great Fire of London,—they were not intended for shops; but, as the requirements of the neighbourhood demanded it, the ground floor of the dwelling-house was transformed into a place of business. In some houses a passage has been left, which allows of a separate entrance to the dwelling-rooms; but more frequently the passage has been joined to the shop; and there is no communication with the upper apartments except through the shop.

If chandlers' shops are bad, those of the butchers are often worse. The accompanying engraving (Fig. 32) represents a characteristic example of the arrangement of many business premises in different parts of the metropolis. A is the cellar, in which are the closet, water-tank, and pickling-tubs; B is the shop; C a small office, which has been built upon what was once a back-yard. This is lighted

Fig. 32.—A Cut through a House in the City.

by one of the skylights to which we have referred. This little apartment has been built out close to the wall of the neighbouring house. E is the kitchen, which is situate, as many City kitchens are, on part of the first floor; D is a sitting-room. The way to these is by a dark, narrow, and inconvenient staircase, leading from the shop. F F are bedrooms. A worse arrangement than this can scarcely be imagined. All the bad air collected in the cellars must pass to the shop; for, except by a small grating in the front, there is no other means of exit.

In a butcher's shop, in the daytime, the unglazed windows admit a good supply of air; and provided that openings are left through to the back, there is sufficient current; but it is not so with some other shops, in which the windows are glazed; and where, often, particularly in cold weather, the door is kept nearly or entirely closed. To return to our illustration. Into such cellars as that shown in the sketch, sheep are pushed down, and other animals slaughtered. We trust, however, that the law which enforces the licensing of slaughter-houses in the metropolis, and their regular inspection, has put a check on such disgraceful practices. Apart from these, however, there is much impurity in such cellars. Some are infested by large rats, which find their way into them from sewers and broken drains; and if the rats can come so, foul air is sure of a passage also.

At night, and during Sundays, the shop is closed by shutters; and at night the skylight is fastened, for fear of thieves. At times, occasionally on Saturday nights, quantities of meat are left unsold; and in the summer, and in dull, heavy weather, it is by no means unusual by the Monday morning to find this stock green, putrid, and quite unfit for food. This material vanishes in the morning; for although it is unsaleable by the butchers, and unfit for food, it notwithstanding finds a market; and we fear is often, in a highly seasoned state, sold in the shape of sausages. This trade should be more closely watched. Now, it is evident that, what with the cellar and what with the shop, those who dwell above are not well placed. The floors of these old-fashioned houses are saturated with grease; and there are other things, such as boxes for waste fat, collecting for the tallow-chandler, which cannot well, under the circumstances, be otherwise preserved, or it would surely be done; for it is evidently to the advantage of the butchers to attend most scrupulously to cleanliness, as nothing sooner taints all kinds of animal food than want of attention in that respect. Some modern butchers' shops are spacious, and thoroughly ventilated: the floors are of stone, and the walls of a polished substance, so that they can be thoroughly washed with water and easily purified. These, however, are exceptions.

To a greater or less extent, the remarks above apply to other shops of a similar construction; and we have been led to make them because, at no great cost, the healthiness of such houses and shops might be much improved. The cellars should be kept scrupulously clean: if it be a necessity that the ashes and dust should be there, a dust-bin with a tight-fitting lid should be fixed, and this should be emptied once or, if it can be done, twice a week: the ground should be flagged; the sinks and closet trapped in the most effectual manner; the front grating enlarged to the greatest possible extent, and the place lime-washed at least four times in the year. This would sweeten the superstructure; and then every means should be used for keeping up a good current of air through the shops, during both night and day. This might be managed to a certain extent by perforated glass in the windows and skylights; by openings at the back, and by open iron gratings over the doors, which might be so constructed as to defy thieves and prevent the admission of rain and snow.

Many architects' and engineers' offices are frequently quite offensive. Now, this is not only selfish, but it is stupid, and quite inconsistent even with an intelligent selfishness; inasmuch as the vigour of the brain depends directly and immediately on the proper aëration of the blood; and if employers could only see or estimate the actual shortcomings and losses to themselves through the want of this, they would probably be more desirous of providing a free supply of that cheap commodity, fresh air, to their assistants than they are. They may depend on it their contempt for such considerations does not show superior sagacity on their parts, but superior ignorance of the inevitable laws of physiology, and of health and vigour of brain and body. In the case of foolish slave-ship captains, who stow their poor slave passengers under close hatches, and kill them by hundreds from want of fresh air, were some intelligent underling to warn any one of them that the want of fresh air was the cause of the deaths, we doubt not he would be snubbed for his impudence, sneered at as a pragmatical and conceited fool, and his advice or entreaty despised; but how evidently it would be for the benefit of the owners, as well as of the slaves, to give the utmost attention to such advice, there are few who cannot see. Why, then, should employers of all kinds be so stupid as they are with respect to the welfare of those the value of whose higher labours is far greater than that of slaves? And although there certainly are masters who care little whether their servants be killed by slow degrees while serving *their* purpose, such masters ought seriously to consider whether their purpose really be best served without regard for the health and vigour of those dependent on them for a livelihood.

In the sanitary arrangement of houses, even for the richer classes, the ventilation of cupboards is neglected. In places let out in tenements, closets are the receptacles for bread and fragments of various other kinds of food. Often the dirty clothes are put away in those places, waiting for washing. It is, therefore, most important that air should be plentifully passed through such corners: generally, however, there is but little arrangement made for this purpose. The doors are kept close, without any perforations. There are no ventilators in the walls, and in consequence those places become cases of polluted air, which, when the doors are opened, escapes over the apartments. This defect is visible in nearly all houses of old date; and while looking at some dwellings of recent construction, it is seen that although care has been generally taken to ventilate staircases and rooms, the cupboards are in this respect neglected. Notwithstanding, in houses which are intended for letting in tenements, this is a matter of considerable importance.

Of the effects of impure air, there is a striking illustration in an interesting little book, written by Miss Goodman, one of the English Sisters of Mercy who rendered good service during the Crimean war. The lady, in giving an account of a deadly nook in the hospital at Scutari, says: "In the midst of those struggling between life and death, as are the inhabitants of hospitals, the baneful effect of causes which render the air impure is more evident, because it is sufficient to turn the balance, and to produce not merely disease, but its fatal issue. A bed in a corridor in which I worked was so situate that its occupant was near the current of a draft of impure air, which, having travelled up a passage, crossed the corridor to escape through a doorway. Of a number of patients—perhaps twenty—who were assigned to this couch, none left it but for their final resting-place. It was at the end of the corridor at which I entered, so that the first face that greeted me each morning would be that of the soldier on the fated bed; then, in a few days, I should have to pass his lifeless body. Again, after a short interval, some new tenant would receive me cheerfully, perhaps remarking, as many of those who arrived did, how happy he felt in being from under canvas, and having a house over his head once more,—with a dash of gallantry, some may say, that it was very comfortable when a man was sick out there to see an English woman. As I stopped I used to feel unable to look the poor fellow in the face: there seemed to be in my heart a fatal secret which I was keeping from him. At length, to my great relief, the bedstead was taken away, and that part of the corridor remained unoccupied."

Deadly beds, somewhat similar to the above, may be met with in some of the hospitals and infirmaries in England at the present day.

Many yards are sources of disease. One day, when hot bright sunshine and storm were fighting for the mastery, we chanced to visit the back part of some premises, which may be taken as a sample of thousands that are still to be found in the metropolis. The yard was partly covered with broken brick pavement, the sink was imperfect, and a cesspool and rotten brick drain stretched underneath part of the ground. When the sun came forth, children began to play in this place. The rooms adjoining were crowded with inhabitants—old and young. The soil, both through the drain and in consequence of what had been thrown on the surface, had become completely polluted, and when the hot rays of the sun beat on the ground, clouds of steam rose from the earth and dispersed abroad. Although not always so clearly seen, the impurities of such a soil are constantly rising, particularly in the summer-time, causing a vast amount of sickness and death. The mention of this may lead some who are in search for a dwelling to keep their eyes open to such points, and perhaps induce others to have faults remedied.

CHAPTER XIII.

TRAVELLERS BY SEA AND LAND.

A FEW pages back we alluded to the want of fresh air on board slave-ships, and the consequent loss of life. This state of things, however, exists in other ships besides slave-ships, and calls loudly for alteration.

It is impossible to reprehend too strongly the miserable and unwholesome accommodation which is provided for those valuable men who act in the merchant service of the country. Of late years, great changes have been made in the sanitary arrangements of the Queen's ships. The washing of bed-covering and clothing is strictly attended to; hammocks, and so forth, are aired at frequent intervals; and provisions are made, sometimes under difficult circumstances, for ventilation. In many merchant ships, no care seems to be taken. During the heat of the last summer, we took an opportunity to examine some north-country colliers and other vessels, in the port of London. Anything worse than the accommodation of the crews can scarcely be conceived. The berths, intended for sleeping-room for two men, were not much larger than coffins; the bedding was not too clean; jackets and overcoats hung about. In parts which were not used for sleeping there were stores of various kinds in lockers, and the limited space was still further occupied by chests and packages (Fig. 33). We all know that space is valuable on shipboard; but this very

Fig. 33.—*A Berth to bring Death.*

circumstance renders necessary the greatest and the most scrupulous care. Great improvements require to be made in the ventilation and arrangements of the sleeping-places in those vessels. Bad as they are, Russian, Prussian, and even French ships, are worse. It is, therefore, not to be wondered at, that we hear every now and then accounts of the outbreak of yellow fever, cholera, and other pestilential disorders, on board ship. Improvements here are loudly called for.

This may lead us to travellers of another kind. With reference to the very poorest class of wayfarers, enactments have been made for the safety of their health and for their general comfort. Unless the drainage be efficient, cleanliness attended to, and a sufficient amount of breathing-space and accommodation provided for each poor traveller, no house is licensed for their reception. There are, however, a very large number of persons whose means are not great, and who, in these railway times, are driven from home by business and other occasions, and who would not for a moment think of going amongst strange bedfellows in the common lodging-houses. It is to be regretted that in many large towns there is not to be found equal accommodation for them at four or five times the cost of the places alluded to.

In most of the large towns there are modern hotels, which are fitted with every convenience after a fashion; but the cost and arrangements of these establishments put them out of the reach of the class of travellers to whom we are referring. In many of the old-fashioned towns, particularly in the north of England, there are inns that have now become of a second, and even lower rate, which are execrable in their sanitary arrangements, but which, for miserable accommodation, charge what is really an exorbitant price. For instance, a traveller whose means compel him to be economical may, at the end of his railway journey, call at an inn whose glory seems to have declined, but whose somewhat snug exterior appearance induces him to think he may be able there to take his ease, without being charged more than he can conveniently pay. He finds, however, in the morning, that although the attendance has been of the worst, his bedroom most unwholesome, the hangings of the old-fashioned four-post bedstead and the paper of the wall faded with time and mildew, the whole interior fittings falling into "the sear, the yellow leaf,"—the bill next morning is :—

	s.	d.
Supper	2	0
Bed	2	6
Breakfast	2	0
Attendance	1	0
	7	6

We have occasionally noted the "dog-holes" in which some travellers who come late are placed. One of these opened from a passage in which there was no light except from a window at the further end. There was a dark narrow staircase, which led to this passage. In the bedrooms on the right-hand side there were no fireplaces or means of ventilation at the back, and the only opening in the front was a door with a small window, which was lighted by the passage-window: on the opposite side were other bedrooms, which, although small, were better circumstanced, for they had windows which looked into the street in front of the premises. We made a sketch of the place, removing a partition to show the inside of one of the rooms, and here it is, with a plan (Fig. 34).

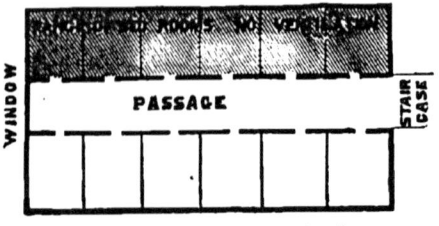

Fig. 34.—*Packing and Poisoning.*

The rooms are very small; and, without taking into account the impurities which usually surround buildings of this description, it is very clear that travellers are worse off for accommodation in places like these than the poorest person is who seeks for shelter in the licensed common lodging-houses. In such situations as this, in buildings chiefly of wood, occupants may reasonably be fearful of a sudden outbreak of fire.

Believing that there is a very great necessity in many provincial towns for accommodation for second and third class travellers, we have taken some trouble, from time to time, to examine the rooms which are provided for their use. In some very large towns—Manchester, for instance; and the same will be found to be the case in many other places—a stranger who requires to stop for a few days, at limited expense, may wander long before he meets with a place suitable for his purpose. There are but few coffee-houses with sufficient bed accommodation. In some instances, near railway stations, large houses have been taken, and, although unfit in their internal arrangements, have been extemporized into coffee-rooms, dining and sleeping places. In these every morsel of space, regardless of health, has been turned to account. Beds are placed in closets, and small rooms barely sufficient for one person are divided by thin partitions into two or three sleeping apartments, in which there is scarcely room to move or breathe. These rooms, bad as they are, are eagerly sought for by persons coming by the late trains, or who may require to start early in the morning. The profits of some of these houses must be enormous.

There is certainly need of interference in connexion with many of the establishments where second and third class travellers are forced to stop, and we see no reason why such places should not be inspected and made wholesome before they are let in this manner.

CHAPTER XIV.

GOOD COOKERY AND BAD COOKERY FOR THE MULTITUDE.

THE unsatisfactory and wasteful system of cooking, or rather want of system, which prevails amongst the industrious and poorer classes of this country, demands reform. In the ill-constructed houses in which thousands of the working population of the metropolis live, the waste in cooking is enormous; and this is caused partly by the unsuitable formation of the fire-places, and partly by want of knowing how to manage.

The practice of filling with several families a house which was intended for only one, prevents the possibility of any proper arrangement for cooking in the kitchens of those houses. There is ample provision for preparing a dinner: there are boilers and ovens which are of daily use to a family, but unfortunately this accommodation is only available for one tenant, the remainder of the persons living in the house being obliged to manage as well as they can with fire-places which were intended only to warm parlours, bedrooms, or drawing-rooms.

We have made a careful sketch in such a room, the truth of which will be recognized by thousands of well-paid artisans and other workers in the metropolis (Fig. 35). The fire-grate is not more than ten and a half inches in width, and in height seven and a quarter inches. In this instance—and it is one of a multitude—there were not more than three or four inches of space on each hob. In order to get the vegetables ready, it is necessary to place the pan in such a position that it covers nearly the whole of the top part of the fire, and this prevents the roasting of the meat, and generally leads the smoke to fill the apartment and cover everything in it with flakes of soot. There is barely room for one pan on the fire at a time, and if potatoes and cabbages are to be made ready for the Sunday's dinner, they must be boiled one after the other, and one vegetable is sure to be spoilt by being kept waiting. Few joints of butcher's meat can be found to fit those wretched cooking-grates. A neck or breast of mutton is far too long, only part of it is touched by the fire at one time; and other joints are equally difficult to manage. It is not to be wondered at, under such circumstances, that the temper of housewives becomes ruffled, and that husbands are glad to get out of the way until dinner-time. Even then matters are not satisfactory: for in nine cases out of ten the food, when put upon the table, is neither pleasant to the sight nor cooked with advantage. Even with fireplaces of this description, good dinners for small families might be cooked with the help of a "Dutch oven," or other contrivance of a similar kind; but these appliances are used by few.

When all this muddle, confusion, smoke, waste, and ill-temper are caused by cooking in a room of this kind, it is not to be wondered at that the bakehouse is extensively patronized on Sundays. Into the public ovens go all kinds

Fig. 35.— Cooking and Wasting.

of meat—pork, beef, mutton, geese, and other matters,—and it is certain that by this process a large amount of the nutritious qualities of the food is wasted, while the flavour of the varieties of butcher's meat must be assimilated.

In various ways the science of cookery has made advances: in workhouses, prisons, and hospitals, the saving which has been effected by improved apparatus, and by the preparation of food on a proper plan and on a wholesale scale, is enormous. The cost per head at which persons can be properly maintained is thus considerably diminished. The articles are obtained from the cheapest and best markets, and everything is put to its proper use with the least waste. In the army, Captain Grant's apparatus, and that of Messrs. Benham & Son, are doing wonders: besides the large sums which they are the means of saving, such improvements tend, in consequence of the soldiers being enabled to obtain a variety of well-cooked food, to improve health and lengthen life.

In some of the public schools a reform of the system of cooking is much required: take, for instance, the Blue Coat School, where, for the most part, the meat is baked, and there is but little variety in the food. On shipboard—particularly in the Royal Navy—there is also room for improvement in this respect. When a ship is at sea, the choice of provisions is chiefly confined to salt meats; but in port there is no necessity for this limit. In several of the old-fashioned taverns in the City the plan of cooking is antiquated and expensive, and there are but few places in which a working man can obtain a good dinner at a cost which he can afford to pay: the consequence is that he is generally obliged to take each day a bundle of provisions that have been cooked at home in the manner to which we have referred, and at dinner-time go to the ill-ventilated tap-room of a public-house, where he must, of course, spend a certain amount on beer for very indifferent accommodation.

Look in what direction you may throughout the metropolis—and the same may be said of the chief of our large provincial towns,—you will find no adequate provision made for well and cheaply feeding a vast portion of the community. And in London especially there is but little opportunity for properly preparing food at home. The advantage of cooking with the aid of proper apparatus, on a large scale, has been proved in various ways besides those to which we have referred. In Lancashire, during the prevalence of the late distress, many useful lessons were learned, and persons have been surprised at the large number who can be fed, by proper management, for a comparatively small sum of money. In Glasgow, a movement has been made, which we look to see followed widely. Already the matter has been taken up in London and in Manchester; and so far as experiments have been made, the fact seems to be established that self-supporting cooking depôts, on a handsome scale, can be maintained for the use of the working classes.

More important, however, than this it is that knowledge on the subject of cooking should become general, and that the means of cooking properly, and with the greatest effect at the least cost, at home, should be brought within reach of larger numbers than is now the case. We have no wish to see the family circle broken up, or any place made more attractive to an Englishman than his own fireside.

Besides the prevention of smoke in washhouses—a matter to which we would direct attention,—the arrangement of those places and their position in connexion with small houses require consideration. In many instances, even where there are opportunities for managing otherwise, the washhouse is made to communicate directly with the living-rooms of the dwelling; and the consequence is that, even with closed doors, it is not easy to keep the smoke and steam from entering the various rooms. This should be avoided, the entrance of the washhouse being made as near as possible to the back-door of the dwelling.

In the washhouses which are attached to the smaller description of dwellings that have been erected during the last forty or fifty years, scarcely any care has been taken to ventilate them. In many instances the small windows are so constructed that they will not open, and there is no outlet except the door and the copper-hole. Even in new houses, and often in those of a good class, this matter has been much neglected. A simple and not very costly remedy for this want of ventilation would be to place a weather-boarded opening on the roof, constructed somewhat similarly to those which we often see on small country breweries.

Very often the washhouse chimney will not give forth smoke at all; but when it does, this is, especially in towns, a cause of much annoyance. The chimneys, being for the most part low, allow the smoke to be blown into the adjoining windows, to dirty the clothes which have been hung to dry, and do other mischief. It is, however, more particularly of the construction of copper stoves and flues in many of these places that we would just now speak. In most instances these can only be cleaned by a complicated machine, and (if a chimney-sweeper is called in) at the cost of half a crown. Some of these copper-stoves always smoke, notwithstanding that they are carefully and regularly swept. We have seen several which become so much congested by the firing needed for three or four days' "washing," that no smoke can pass up at all, lodgments being made in a manner somewhat similar to that which takes place in the chambers of a lamp-black manufactory. The accompanying sketch is no exaggeration, and many a housewife in London and elsewhere will acknowledge the unpleasant faithfulness of the picture (Fig. 36). Some are obliged to lift the copper out entirely every third washing-day, and sometimes oftener, and clear the soot from an elbow of the flue, which cannot be reached in any other way. Others have to blow up with gunpowder every washing-day.

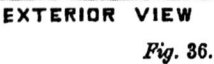

There are scores of wash-houses in which women labour in vain, endeavouring to wash clothes clean in a dense atmosphere of smoke. Instead of the fire acting properly, the smoke comes into the room by the grate and the openings round the door of the copper, for the want of a clear draught. In some instances, the flues of these fireplaces are passed into a neighbouring chimney; but this has generally an unsatisfactory result, though to a certain extent it prevents the ill effects of the short chimneys to which we have referred. There can be no doubt that a great extent of reform is required in the construction of copper flues and fireplaces; thousands of old ones need alteration; and care should be taken in building new ones, that they may not be the means of creating the nuisance of which we complain. No one but those who have had the painful experience can tell the trial which a smoky washhouse brings to the temper, and how much it adds to the general misery of the "washing-day" in the homes of a large number of the more affluent of artizans, and also of many of the middle class. The children look with dread to those times, and the husband gets as far away from the place as possible.

In houses which are inhabited by several families this evil is multiplied; for, supposing there are four families in the house, and that it is the custom for each to have a washing-day, there are four days of smoke and steam instead of one; and this is a matter of consequence when the washhouse is within the dwelling. Here, then, we have an extensive nuisance which requires remedy. No doubt in many instances there are carelessness and want of attention on the part of tenants, but there are thousands of cases in which the greatest care would be unavailing, the original construction is so thoroughly bad.

CHAPTER XV.

FRESH AIR IN THE COUNTRY.

"I AM going out of town for change of air. The wear and tear of London life, the foul Thames, the evil condition of neighbouring streets, are all against me here." Quite true. But take care where you go, or you may jump out of the frying-pan into the fire. And what we said to our friend in particular, we say to our readers in general. Towns are becoming everywhere more and more crowded. In 1801 the rural population of Great Britain amounted to 8,143,722; in 1851, this section of the population had amounted to 13,914,768, showing an increase, in fifty years, of 5,770,996, or 70 per cent., whereas the population of towns of upwards of 20,000 inhabitants, which was in 1801 2,435,184, had risen in 1851 to 7,044,709, an increase of 4,609,525, or 189 per cent. This shows that in the course of half a century the increase of the urban population in proportion to the suburban was about $2\frac{1}{2}$ to 1, and these figures by no means indicate the full extent of the proportionate decrease of the rural part of the population.

When we consider this vast increase in the number of inhabited houses, which have been very nearly doubled during the last half-century, that the population of England and Wales has more than doubled, and that the chief increase of the population is in the towns, the necessity for sanitary regulation, of an enlightened and sufficient nature, is evident, and the usefulness of getting away into the country is no less so. But simply "to go into the country" is not enough. The neighbourhood must be looked at, and circumstances considered. If you send your children to an ill-drained watering-place, and let them play half the day at the mouth of a drain on the beach, or to a damp farmyard, with decomposing vegetable matter on all sides of them, and bad water to drink, the chances are that evil and not good will result. Pure air is the first necessity, and man does all he can to increase the difficulty of obtaining it. Dr. Angus Smith, who has devised means of learning the relative amount of decaying animal and vegetable matter existing in the air under different circumstances, found, as compared with the purest air he examined—that of Lake Lucerne,—that at the forest near Chamounix the amount of the organic matter was double, evidently owing to the decay of the leaves; in North Lancashire, the same. In the fields near large towns, as London and Manchester, there is between nine and ten times as large a quantity as at Lucerne. In the purest parts of London there is double as much as in the adjacent country; although this is immediately reduced one-half by the purifying influence of a thunder-storm. Over the putrid Thames, in the warm weather, there is double the amount of that in the purer parts of London, and four times as much as in the Highgate fields. Manchester is nearly as bad. In close dwelling-houses the air is still worse; and in open pigsties it is so charged with putrifying effluvia, that there is absolutely eighty times the amount of it that is found in the pure air of Lake Lucerne.

If it be correct that, when respiration is performed naturally, there are about 18 respirations in one minute, 1,080 in the hour, and 25,920 in the 24 hours, and that by each respiration a pint of air is sent into the lungs, that is 18 pints in a minute, or in the hour more than two hogsheads, and in the 24 hours more than 57 hogsheads, the effect impurity may produce is evident.

Simple assertions of the evils to which people expose themselves in the country have little effect. A special instance, however, may have more. Our sketch (Fig. 37) shows part of a village in Essex where the houses drain into a large pond on the opposite side of the road. At the time of our visit it was sufficiently foul to produce a pestilence, and we were not surprised to learn that fever frequently visits the cottages, and that the prevailing odours are not those of Araby the blest.

Go into the country by all means for fresh air; but do not take for granted that you will get it.

Many of the ponds situate near farmhouses, and in the centre of villages, often a source of sickness and death, might be abolished, and no inconvenience would ensue. In situations where there is no regular supply of water laid on, it may be said they are needed for the watering of cattle, and for other purposes; but, even in these places, in a majority of cases, troughs, communicating with the sources which supply the ponds, would answer all the purposes required.

Besides the damage to health which is caused by these accumulations of stagnant water, they are but too likely to be hurtful to the horses and cows themselves who drink it. In many of the pleasant villages which skirt the metropolis, the horse-ponds remain, some of them in a shocking condition: these might with great advantage be filled up, horse-troughs might be supplied, and the site of the ponds properly planted and converted into village-greens. Although the pool at Highgate is not so dirty as others, it may be taken as an example of an old fashion, of unsanitary nature, being allowed to exist after the need for it has ceased.

Fig. 37.—Sweetening the Air of the Country. A Village in Essex.

In one week, four deaths from malignant diphtheria occurred in the sub-district of Lewisham, of which three were in one family, an innkeeper's, at a place called Southend. The local registrar states that five deaths have occurred in the same family within a fortnight; and the mother who had suffered such a severe loss informed the registrar that, about two months ago, a part of a large pond, near the house, had been emptied; and that, when the same pond was cleansed about two years ago, typhus raged to a frightful extent in Southend, which contains about three hundred persons; and that as many as forty in that small population had been affected by it. The condition of this pond should be looked into; perhaps it may be found that sewage, or other dangerous matter, passes into it.

A proper consideration of collections of stagnant water should be given by the officers whose duty it is to watch over the public health, not only in the suburbs of the metropolis, but throughout the rural districts. Often ponds are formed in disused gravel and clay pits, and are left open from sheer carelessness; although, by a little contrivance, the rubbish necessarily taken from another part might be as well shot into such holes as elsewhere.

If it had been possible in the old coaching and stage-waggon days for the metropolis to have reached its present proportions, the state of things would have been unbearable; but Providence leads man to accommodate himself to circumstances, so that, by the use of railways and other means of transit, a great part of the population has spread over suburban districts; and now the pent-up Londoner can, at moderate cost, breathe the pure air and enjoy the clear sky and sunny landscape.

As we get away by the Thames from London city, and its smoke and impurities, the tints of the sky change, and the air becomes more wholesome where not interfered with. Accident once led us to another Southend, the social and sanitary arrangements of which are, unfortunately, most deplorable. A brief glance will show that in this population, of about 15,000 persons, there exist a power of evil and source of contamination which are perhaps not to be equalled in the midst of the same number of people in the kingdom. Here, particularly in the Blue Town, as one portion of Sheerness is called, Vice walks with shameless effrontery. Several of the houses are hotbeds of depravity and a means of contamination. The police act with ability and intelligence, and carry out as well as they can the regulations which they have the power of enforcing; but these are insufficient.

From Sheerness, the pleasant little Kentish town of Sittingbourne, about eight miles distant, is soon reached by railway. This small rural town contains, with the parts immediately surrounding, a population of about 6,000, and is admirably situate for all purposes of health: it is, notwithstanding, neglected in a sanitary point of view, as are hundreds of other places.

In most of the large cities and towns, attempts (which are unluckily, in certain instances, inadequate) have been made to establish some system of drainage and water-supply; but an inspection of several of the smaller places shows that nothing is being done there, and that life is sacrificed where it should be safe.

Sittingbourne is chiefly composed of a very long street, with here and there certain back slums and lanes, lined with small houses, leading from it. The main street is well raised above an extensive plain; and fresh wholesome air sweeps from the sea and in other directions. The place also abounds in springs of what should be excellent water. Formerly there was a great traffic of coaches and post-carriages through the town; but this has been stopped by the introduction of railways; and, in consequence, the large inn-yards, which were capable of accommodating many horses, are now either disused or devoted to other purposes. In some, small houses, which are occupied by working people, have been built. There is still some traffic along the road; but persons refer to bygone days, when hundreds of carriages daily passed that way, and the place was lively with the bugle-horn of the coach-guards and the rattling of horses.

There are pleasant old-fashioned gardens attached to some of the better sort of houses, which are well stocked with fruit-trees, and gay with roses and seasonable flowers, backed by the dense dark green foliage which is peculiar to the county of Kent. Round about the town, in parts, are cherry-trees and orchards. All these are matters of enjoyment for persons who are obliged to live for the chief part in London. There is, however, a less agreeable side of the picture: for in many of the houses there is that dense, oppressive, and dangerous atmosphere which arises from cesspools and the want of drainage. In certain instances, on the occasion of our visit, the cesspools were found neglected and overflowing; heaps of refuse had been allowed to remain close to houses; and other matters were left which have the effect of poisoning the air, and, as a natural consequence, by filling the soil with impurities, spoil the water in the wells, on which the inhabitants depend for their daily use. In the western part of Sittingbourne there is a remarkable head of what ought to be the purest and finest water. In a sort of hollow roadway, within the distance of about one hundred and fifty yards, there are numerous springs, from which the water gushes forth in immense quantities, and soon forms a considerable stream. There is here enough water, probably, for the supply of the town, if it were raised to a proper position. It is painful to see how this bountiful provision of one of the main necessaries of life is used. At one part there is an extensive piggery, from which the refuse passes into the water: in another there is a steep hill of soil, which at the bottom mixes with the spring (Fig. 38).

Fig. 38.—Poisoning the Springs: Sittingbourne.

What has been said respecting the sanitary state of Sittingbourne applies to many other places; and it is much to be desired that more attention should be given to the drainage and water-supply of small towns than is at present shown.

Notes have been recently published of many cottage-dwellings which may be taken as a fair example of the houses of a large part of the industrious classes in the country, where we find instances of the most gross sanitary neglect, and arrangements, by existing circumstances forced upon the people, which set all the rules of decency at defiance.

From Norwich we have accounts of places in which ventilation seems to have been altogether neglected: in others it is quite insufficient. In one small cottage of two rooms, occupied by a couple of families consisting of nine persons, the only means of ventilation is a casement one foot wide and two feet in height. In other instances, walls need propping up; in some are rents and cracks; filthy dykes, full of stagnant drainage-matter; and most of the other evils which neglect and ill-construction produce, attend the dwellings provided for an industrious population. It is impossible, during either the night or day, to prevent the admixture of young people of both sexes. Windows are stuffed with rags, floors are full of holes, roofs are leaking, and the plaster and walls are in a shattered condition. But this state of things is now so generally understood, that it would seem scarcely necessary to enter into details.

How can we expect, under such unfortunate circumstances, that our peasantry will be "*their country's pride*"? It is not in the district of Norwich alone that this terrible state of things is allowed. In Bedfordshire, Hertfordshire, Buckinghamshire, and other counties, in which a large part of the population is engaged in agricultural pursuits, matters will be found as bad, if not worse; and it is to be observed, that these are the dwellings chiefly occupied by married workers and their children; and that there are many unmarried men and women, who are accommodated with sleeping-space in the premises of the farmers, who are not better off than those above referred to.

In parts of Yorkshire, portions of Durham, and in Northumberland, the cottage dwellings are of large size and better built than those in the southern counties; but, notwithstanding, there is a sad want of proper plans adapted to the use of an increasing family: here are to be found, in various directions, the most wretched hovels. On the estates of the Duke of Northumberland and elsewhere, during recent years, a marked improvement has been made; but farther northward there are villages to be met with which are not better circumstanced than those which were to be found in this country in the Middle Ages.

It is not, however, in connexion with the houses of the agricultural classes alone that there is reason for complaint. Throughout the mining districts of Northumberland and Durham there is also great need for improvement. "*The Pit Raws*" (rows) are mostly long ranges of dwellings, of only a single story in height. In front of each house there is generally a door and a single window. The front room is usually of fair dimensions, in which the family live, and where part of them sleep. The inner room is of smaller size, and is neatly and well furnished. This is used for sleeping in, and on Sundays, or important occasions, for the reception of visitors. For the most part, there are in these houses no sculleries or accommodation for washing clothes, and this work must therefore be done in the principal room—or, when the weather is fine, in front of the house. Behind each of these buildings there is usually a garden. In some there are privies, with cesspools, which are often rudely constructed by the pitmen themselves; but, in a multitude of instances, *there is no provision of this kind at all.*

To a considerable extent, paving and draining are neglected.* In front of the houses are dust-heaps, mostly uninclosed, on which all household refuse is thrown. Near these there is generally a pigsty; and it seems to be a remarkable circumstance, that while the gardens are well kept, and the interiors of the houses beautifully neat, the furniture brightly polished, the bedding well attended to,—while the men and boys after their work take care to wash themselves clean, and the women are particular as regards neat and tidy dress, they should, notwithstanding, cause such unsightly accumulations before their own doors, which are as indecent as they are unpleasant and dangerous. But the people themselves are not altogether to blame for this, for we do not see how, with the present arrangement of a majority of the dwellings of this kind, it is altogether to be avoided.

These pit rows are usually the property of the owners of particular collieries, to whom it is customary for the men and boys to bind themselves for a stated period, and for certain considerations: part of the latter is the possession of a house, rent free, with coals, and sometimes candles; and in this way the workpeople are entirely dependent on their employers for the construction of their homes.

* At Killingworth Colliery Village, a black open ditch passes at no great distance from the front of the houses. This carries off part of the surface water, but is in itself a source of poison.

This very important matter, which affects a vast and industrious multitude, was brought under the notice of the British Association, at Newcastle; and it is hoped that the need of change which was then shown will lead to beneficial results, and that at an early day the Marchioness of Londonderry, the Earl of Durham, Lord Ravensworth, Mr. Matthew Bell, and other large colliery proprietors, who derive enormous revenues from this trade, will strive in a worthy spirit of rivalry for the removal of an evil which is disgraceful to themselves, and stops the right progress of the persons whom they employ.

The dwellings of this class are provided for the most part, as we have said, by the masters: the men have no choice in the matter. It is therefore clear that the employers are responsible for the fashion and condition of these places; and they might, if they would, easily put a stop to middens and other abominations in front of the dwellings.

Many of the rows are built on sites which are quite unsuitable, where it is next to an impossibility to provide, if even the disposition were shown, any sort of drainage. This, it is said, is caused by the necessity which exists for having the homes of the men near their work, and so preventing them from being under the necessity of walking long distances, often in the night-time, to and from the pit. It is also stated that a limited space of land only, round the pit's mouth, being the property of the coal-owner, has been made use of, when a better site, at no great distance off, might have been obtained at a little extra cost. Generally, in the neighbourhood of the coal-pits, the land is barren, and of small worth for agricultural purposes, the richness of the bowels of the earth atoning for the nakedness of the surface. Supposing that the sties and middens were removed from the front to the rear, part of the space in the front might, if it were of any use, be railed off; and, as an equivalent, a roadway made along the gardens at the back of the row, which would allow the passage of carts for the removal of refuse when necessary. This done, the casting of filth in front of the rows should be strictly forbidden. Then, to some extent in the front of the cottages, the space should be paved. Spouts should be provided for carrying the rain-water into covered casks, where it would be useful for washing and other purposes.

Drainage is indispensable, and scavengers are necessary in even the best constructed of the pit-rows. It must not be forgotten that within a short distance of the Earl of Durham's residence, in Lambton Park, cholera carried off hundreds of people.

We have made a drawing of one of the pit-rows, to show their evils, exaggerating nothing (Fig. 39).

Fig. 39.—Pitmen's Dwellings in the North. A Refining Prospect.

CHAPTER XVI.

WINDOW GARDENS, AND GARDEN SHOWS.

A MOVEMENT has taken place in certain metropolitan parishes, to encourage the culture of flowers and plants in such situations as can be found for this purpose; and it is gratifying to find that, in consequence of the success which has attended the first attempts, efforts are being made in other directions for a similar promotion of the means of adding a beauty to the homes of the poor. Much is to be done in this way, even under difficult circumstances, where there is an inclination.

As an instance, we give a sketch (Fig. 40), made on the spot, near Cripplegate Church, London, Milton's neighbourhood, and which in his day was famed for pleasant houses and gardens. Now the population has become dense, and, for the most part, poor; and the greenery has almost vanished. Our view shows an attempt to bring the freshness of the country into a dark and smoky region of the town. The site of this garden is the flat part of the roof of a small outhouse or washhouse. A window of a room opens upon it. The apartment is occupied by a poor woman; and in the spring-time it is surprising to notice, although the brightness of

Fig. 40.—A Window Garden.

Hatfield or Blenheim is not to be found, how pleasant these flowers look by contrast with what is around. The means are very humble. A large bushy wallflower is planted in part of an old butter-tub; in a common wooden box, a hollyhock is coming up; in an old cracked red jar, which has been obtained from some Italian warehouse, is a lilac,—small and sickly, it must be confessed; near the window is a mignonette-box; and in a cracked teapot are some stocks. There is southern-wood, in fair condition; a creeping plant, which forms a shade round the window; a *fleur-de-lis*, and some other flowers. "And, sir," said the gardener, "notwithstanding the cold, I have had some primroses this season." This scene, which, while it is pleasant, is rather touching, is improved by the notes of the blackbird that hangs in its cage against the wall. A little boy near said that, in the mornings, it sang so well, that it was almost as good as being in Highgate Woods; and as the song of this bird could be heard at a considerable distance, it would not be easy to say how many thoughts of other and pleasanter places might be brought by it to the minds of neighbours. A taste similar to what we show here might be very extensively cultivated, particularly amongst the children of the national schools, and with good effect.

The body and the spirits are alike improved by the cultivation of a garden. It offers an enjoyment for which no one is too high or too low. More grows in the cotter's plot than flowers: the cultivation of pansies may tend to his heart's ease; the bed of thyme may speed a dull hour; and kind thoughts may spring up while watering the clump of forget-me-nots. Everywhere the heart of man blesses flowers: the child seeks them in the hedges; the old man finds, in their culture and study, soothing recreation and delight; Pagan and Christian have used them in their rites: flowers deck the bride, and are strewn on the grave. In every country they smile around us; to every grade they offer enjoyment; they give additional beauty to the new palace; they lovingly shroud the decaying ruin. Babylon had its hanging-gardens; Greece its roses and lilies,—

"*Lilia mista Rosis;*"

and Rome its box-trees cut into the figures of animals, ships, and letters; to say nothing of its violets and crocuses. Our first parents, indeed, came into the world in a garden, and Milton makes Eve say as amongst her griefs,—

———"O Flowers,
My early visitation and my last
At even, which I had bred up with tender hand
From the first opening bud, and gave ye names,
Who now shall rear ye to the sun, or rank
Your tribes, and water from the ambrosial fount?"

The ancients had a different idea of horticultural beauty from ours, if we may judge from a passage in Plutarch, quoted by Dr. William Smith, where he speaks of the practice of setting off the beauties of roses and violets, by planting them side by side with leeks and onions, a passage which has been thought to give a proof that flowers were cultivated more to be used for garlands than to beautify the garden.

Cottage Garden societies might be made the means of spreading a knowledge of the best modes of cultivation to all parts of the land. This has not been sufficiently attended to yet. Some plan might be devised for supplying, at moderate price, seeds and plants of the most approved kinds. It requires no more labour to grow the best than the worst sorts; but, as a general rule, cottagers, and often those far above them in the social scale, go on perpetuating the kinds of apples, pears, gooseberries, or currants which their fathers cultivated before them, instead of the improved, and equally hardy, and often far more productive varieties which have since been introduced.

It is interesting to notice the extent to which gardening has grown. In 1403, the chief products of our gardens were cabbages, onions, and garlic. Apple, pear, cherry, and quince trees seem to have been the only fruit-trees in England at that time. The plum-tree was first introduced into this country in 1580, being brought from Asia. The cockspur hawthorn was first cultivated here in 1692. The maple-leaved hawthorn was introduced into England from America in the year 1738. A beautiful variety of the alder was first cultivated in England in the year 1780, being brought from Switzerland, Siberia, and other cold countries. The cedar was first cultivated here in 1664, and the common white larch, which now covers with such excellent effect so many wild parts of the kingdom, but is becoming diseased, was accidentally taken to Scotland in 1737. Mr. Menzies, of Culdare, having procured four of these plants from Siberia, gave two to the Duke of Atholl, which are still in full vigour at Dunkeld, and may be called the parents of all the larch-trees in the kingdom. The mulberry-tree was introduced in the reign of James I. The lime is said to have been brought into England by the Romans; but it does not appear to have been planted in Scotland before the reign of Charles II. The general cultivation of carrots, it is said, originated with certain Flemings who fled hither in the reign of Queen Elizabeth, and settled at Sandwich, in Kent. Peas were a rarity in that same reign. They were brought from Holland. Fuller speaks of them as "fit dainties for ladies: they came so far and cost so dear." The opinions which prevail in respect of some flowers are curious. The snap-dragon, for example, is thought by the less advanced people in some countries to exercise supernatural influence—to have the power of destroying charms and baffling maledictions. Bachelors' buttons are viewed as having a magical effect on the fortunes of lovers. How oddly, too, have some plants reached us. Saffron, which was at one time cultivated to such an extent in Essex as to give its name to a town, came to us from abroad at the risk of a life. Hakluyt was told at Saffron Walden that a pilgrim brought from the Levant to England, in the reign of Edward III., the first root of saffron, which he had found means to conceal in his staff, made hollow for that purpose. "If he had been taken, by the law of the country from whence it came, he had died for the fact." Saffron Hill, Holborn, part of Ely Gardens, had its name from the crops it bore.

Fashion alone produces constant changes in our floriculture. The hollyhock was nearly banished by the dahlia, and is found, even now, more's the pity, oftener in the cottager's garden than in the dress ground of the squire. It is to be hoped the cottar will not give it up, and that the squire will take it back; indeed, there is evidence that he is doing so. What can be finer than a varied group of them, pillars of brilliant colours, against an old stone wall, or clump of dark shrubs? The most gorgeous bit of garden colour we can remember to have seen was a front garden thus fitted up, near Wilton, in

Wiltshire. The dahlia, we may mention, which comes from Mexico, and is named after Dahl, a Swede, was brought into fashion by Lady Holland, at Holland House, Kensington, in 1804. The English are peculiarly favoured in being able to cultivate, thanks to climate and science, nearly every description of plant. The wonderful orchid from Mexico, the moss from Iceland, the creeper from Indian jungle, can alike be made to flourish in this country. However, what we have chiefly in view just now are the flowers—

"That dwell beside our paths and homes,"

the pleasures they afford, and the means of extending these enjoyments. In the vicinity of populous towns, advantages would arise from proprietors letting small portions of land to their less fortunate neighbours for garden purposes, in which the wives and children might assist. We can speak positively as to the benefits of such a system, and of how many kindly feelings it is the producer. We would have the enjoyments of the garden made as general as possible. We do not ask for an Isola Bella, where a barren rock, manured with gold, is made to bloom with bays and orange-trees, or *Louis Quatorzième* expanses with fountains and statues, and delusive perspectives, the glories of Blenheim and Stowe, or even gardens after the "grand manner" of Batty Langley, much abused of men. We plead but for the simplest enclosure and the homeliest flowers. How much is the family tie strengthened by the daisy necklace strung in infancy, and the after-life brightened with the recollection of chaplets of wild flowers woven for saucy faces in early life. It has been said too, and wisely, that "if you are poor, yet modestly aspiring, keep a vase of flowers on your table, and they will help to maintain your dignity, and secure for you consideration and delicacy of behaviour." For the same reason, it is not surprising to learn what they who have been in the habit of awarding prizes in various parishes say,— and it is this, that in almost every instance where they have found a good garden, they have observed that the woman, the children, and the house, were also neat, orderly, and well kept. We need not seek a better reason for advocating the establishment of a Cottage Garden association in every village where there is not one already.

We have crept from the town to the country, from the filthy dens in which men, women, and children are brutalized and destroyed, to the spirit-raising and blood-purifying garden, and we will not return to dirt, damp, darkness, degradation, disease, and death. We ask, with as much solemn earnestness as we may venture to assume, for attention to the miserable state of things set forth, and for as much aid as can be obtained to effect an improvement. This is no mere word-mongering; no book-making: it is, in all sincerity and seriousness, what it professes to be—A BLOW FOR LIFE.

THE END.

From Reviews of previous Works by the Author on the same subject.

From THE ATHENÆUM.

"When our old travellers, in their methodical way, undertook to describe the state and manners of any strange tribe with whom they came in contact, they always laid great stress, though apparently unconscious of the importance of their task, on the size, form, furniture, and general economy of houses, hovels, or huts. They felt instinctively that scarcely any better mode existed of marking the stage of civilisation at which a people had arrived than by describing the places where the chief part of its inactive life is passed. As naturalists divine the habits of a bird or a beast from its nest or den, so can we predicate much, and with certainty, of a man whose habitation we have examined, whose bed we have seen, whose cupboard we have opened. Mr. Godwin boldly says, 'homes are the manufactories of men.' There is something startling in the assertion; but it is in the main true. Take a human being, from whatever situation of life, and place him for a given number of years in a 'home' such as we find painted in this little volume, and there will be a great change observable. The change will not only be physical, but mental. There is a connexion mysterious, but undeniable, between dirt, disease, and crime. To expect to meet with correct notions of morality, as a general rule, in the lanes, alleys, courts, dens, and rookeries which Mr. Godwin describes with so much faithfulness and vigour, would be absurd; and we are not surprised to find that, after having convinced himself and his readers that there are in London immense numbers of people who live under conditions in which virtue is impossible, he should add this pregnant sentence, 'It seems almost an injustice to punish for a natural result.' Few will meditate on such a suggestion without fruit.

Mr. Godwin has not written from vague reports, but has himself *travelled* in London in search of facts and illustrations. With a courage and a patience that cannot be too highly commended, he has explored all the more remarkable haunts of poverty in the metropolis. There are places worse than even he describes; but his object was not to study the strongholds of crime and mendicancy, but to ascertain in what kind of habitations the more unfortunate members of the working classes are located. He found it difficult, as might have been expected, to draw the line. There are circumstances under which the workman who would be honest is driven under the same roof, into the same room even, with the tramp or the pickpocket. Is not this a dangerous state of things? Mr. Godwin, who thinks practically, says it is both dangerous and expensive. We cannot afford to allow it to continue if there be any possible remedy; and, instead of wasting time in attending to those strange theorists who attribute the increase of crime to the spread of intellectual cultivation, it is better to be persuaded at once that, if crime increases, it is because, from want of due care and forethought in those having influence, there exist vast masses of men living with their wives and families in forced communion with the outcasts of society. There is another point on which Mr. Godwin insists, almost equally important. The 'Homes of the Thousands' are not healthy,—not adapted in any way to favour the continuance of life. They are ill ventilated, ill protected from wind and weather, wretchedly provided with the most necessary accessories to human dwelling-places, and, above all, miserably deficient in means of cleanliness. In many cases the water-butts are empty all Sunday; in others the deficiency is so continual that the poor people absolutely 'thank God for a fire' because it gives them an opportunity of obtaining a copious supply of water. Surely these matters are worth considering. If it be important, from economical motives, to diminish the chances of the spread of crime, it is equally important, from sanitary motives, to diminish the chances of the spread of disease. The pestilence generated on the banks of the Fleet River may reach the classes who pride themselves on the salubrious situation in which they live. Selfishness is not only odious,—it is positively the worst form of imprudence. 'When every man is his own end, all things will come to a bad end,' says Coleridge, quoted by Mr. Godwin. We are all interested in removing the evils so ably described in this volume. It is written in a most practical spirit—a spirit at once wise and kind—and should be extensively circulated. The lesson that it inculcates—one of wide application—is, that no man is safe so long as others are uncomfortable."

From THE ART JOURNAL.

"There is ample food for melancholy meditation in Mr. Godwin's little book, and an ample field set forth for the labours of the Christian and the philanthropist in the work of ameliorating the condition of those classes of our countrymen and countrywomen to which its pages refer. It seems almost incredible—and is enough to damp the energies of the most ardent regenerator of those whom we call the 'masses'—that so much of vice and misery should still exist, notwithstanding the vast efforts that have been made within the last few years for their suppression: evils are put down in one place, only to rise up in greater numbers and strength at another, so that the only chance of ultimate and lasting improvement seems to be the united action of all in a position better than those whom it is designed to benefit. Individual interference, and that of societies, have done much; but infinitely more than has been already accomplished is still undone. On reading over Mr. Godwin's fearful narrative, one is well-nigh tempted to ask whether a curse does not rest upon a city where such iniquity and such squalor prevail without any universal attempts being made to eradicate them root and branch. 'Verily, we are guilty concerning our brother.'"

From BELL'S MESSENGER.

"A work like this ought to circulate by tens of thousands of copies, since it points out the misery and wretchedness of the poorer districts of our cities and large towns, and indicates the means for the amelioration of the unhappy condition of the masses. Would that our legislators would turn their attention to practical sanitary measures! Nothing, however, seems to move them. When the Thames stinks, so as to be unbearable, then the House of Commons holds its nose, and vows that something must be done—but that something is never done, leading politicians preferring to squabble for place, rather than to benefit the populations, who are totally unfit for the franchise, so long as they are content to rot in the slough of filth and demoralization, which foul homes and fouler habits engender. Mr. Godwin shows, indeed, that civilisation and progress can make no strides whilst such a state of dirt prevails, even within a stone's throw of the dwellings of the wealthiest, to which dwellings they never give a thought. Mr. Godwin is a gentleman who is not to be deterred from his philanthropic exertions by the stubbornness of aldermen, or the ignorance of overseers, churchwardens, and common councilmen. Nevertheless, his task in striving to promote sanitary reform is one of colossal magnitude, which nothing short of a plague seems likely to accomplish. Things in this country only advance by slow degrees; and therefore Mr. Godwin must be content to bide his time. That he will eventually succeed, we have no more doubt than that we are now giving him all the credit he deserves for his unmitigated perseverance in the true paths of benevolence and civilization; but we fear he must bide his time, and again and again enforce the truths which he has so sensibly and practically enumerated in this volume of fearful facts and discreditable indifference respecting the

Reviews of previous Works by the Author on the same subject.

homes and habits of the poor, before he will be able to bring his purpose to a successful issue."

From THE MORNING POST.

"The prevalence of disease and precocity of vice among the lower classes in London are subjects which force themselves from time to time on public attention. Ravages of cholera or some fearful exhibitions of depravity proclaim the existence of evils ominous of greater mischiefs yet in store. Alarmed affluence sets on foot a feeble scheme of amendment; but, as the question involves neither the interests of a party nor the preponderance of a sect, as soon as the immediate danger has passed away the zeal of remedy flags and subsides again into inert indifference. The want of a practical education and industrial training adapted to the condition and station of each individual is felt to be the radical cause of this abnormal social state. Benevolence occasionally sends forth through the press an indignant protest or earnest appeal, but has hitherto failed to excite that vigorous application of redundant means which wealth can command and the emergency requires. A few years ago the able author of the work now before us published 'a small volume' called 'London Shadows: a Glance at the Homes of the Thousands.' In this he showed how 'thousands of our countrymen and countrywomen are condemned to exist in this metropolis in dens where cleanliness is impossible, and health and morals are alike speedily degraded; where children are educated downwards, and made criminals, with little fault of their own.' His statements made some impression, the sympathies of periodicals were manifested in valuable articles; the titled and the opulent were startled by his 'horrible truths;' but the public were not aroused from their 'foolish and wicked apathy,' till a few months afterwards the cholera again broke out; in the very district which he had taken for the first illustration of his work, the neighbourhood of Berwick-street and Broad-street, Golden-square, this frightful visitation carried nearly 700 persons to their graves in a few days. Alarm was then excited. Sanitary measures have since been adopted. We have seen in the 'Lost Link' what private exertions are effecting by home missions, which carry instruction and relief into the abodes of misery. But this is comparatively little; the amendment produced bears but a small proportion to the wider scope for mischief which increasing population offers. The author has therefore followed up his former publication by this 'Sequel,' to show the present state of London and its vicinity. The districts are described from personal inspection, and views of the most prominent nuisances are given, to place them distinctly before the eye. It is not merely in the narrow streets and close courts of ancient parishes that disease is engendered; the newest domiciles are often erected in situations where salubrity is carelessly and criminally neglected. An instance of this is seen in Canning-town, recently built on the Plaistow Marshes, where long streets, with houses, shops, taverns, and churches, are planted seven feet below the high-water level of the Thames, and are protected from daily inundation only by frail embankments. We shudder while we follow this useful guide into all the haunts of natural and moral corruption which lie around us; the swamp which taints by its blasts of pestilence the air we breathe, and the schools of vice where future thieves and murderers are trained in prurient infamy; these are so faithfully depicted that they ought to arouse one simultaneous effort to avert calamities which wear such a threatening aspect. If philanthropy be too cold to prompt, self-preservation might sound the alarm."

From THE BRISTOL TIMES.

"Though this work has a figurative name, it portrays, with strong, and broad, and practical pencil, terrible realities, which it behoves us, if for no better reason, for that of self-preservation, not to turn away from, or go by on the other side to avoid them. The Levite could do this with the poor smitten traveller, without any fear of the neglected man rising up to punish that neglect; but we cannot calculate upon entire impunity, if we adopt this course with the myriads residing in wretchedness, and ignorance and vice, in what are called 'the back slums' of those human hives, our great towns and cities. We cannot ignore them; they will not let us. They will not stay in their dark haunts—we cannot keep them there: but they will come forth and make reprisals upon society for society's great sin in disowning them; they will react upon their deserters—

'As heaps of dead
Will slay their slayers by the pest they spread.'

'Town Swamps and Social Bridges,' which it must have cost not only considerable mental labour to write, but much personal exertion—much hard and harrowing labour —to obtain the materials for it, is a sequel to another by the same able author, called 'London Shadows: a Glance at the Homes of the Thousands,' which showed that thousands of our countrymen and countrywomen are condemned to exist in the metropolis, in dens where cleanliness is impossible, and health and morals are alike speedily degraded; where children are educated downwards, and made criminals with little fault of their own. There are (as Mr. Godwin has shown) in 'the depths of the shadows lying here, there, and everywhere, at the back of the bright thoroughfares where fashion disports itself— the festers and malignant sores with which the body of society is spotted, though they are carefully hidden away.' As society will not go and see for itself, Mr. Godwin, careless of trouble and offence, and, we may say, of danger, has gone and seen for society, and made his report —and an awful report it is. It requires a strong head to look down into the black abyss (which he has discovered, and proposes to bridge over) of wretchedness, of evil, of want, of wickedness, yet all not less to be pitied than condemned. Yet painful as the subject is, it is fascinating, and Mr. Godwin has contrived to tell his narrative—to give the result of his researches in such a way that, though he makes you *feel*, he does not repel you. The topic is in itself so sad and harrowing, it requires no dressing up, and Mr. Godwin avoids, with good taste and judgment, all meretricious aid to increase the tragic effect. In as pleasant a tone, too, as a man may speak on such matters, he speaks to you. We hope, nay, we believe, his book will have good effect; at all events he deserves every credit for it."

From THE LEADER.

"Mr. Godwin, of the *Builder*, is a man to be honoured. His first taste has been for art, and his labours have seconded a love of what is natural and beautiful, in every way, and to use happily a pleasant pen has been his duty for years. Yet he steps from the sphere of such quiet duties, to encounter the ugliest and most unwholesome terrors of London. He goes about doing good. He has been among the dens of Agar-town and the courts round Drury-lane, and in many another place where dirt abounds, and he goes to show why pure abundant water should refresh homes squalid for its want, and how the cheerful light of day should be made to pierce into dark cellars and reeking yards. He has chosen to preach the virtue next to godliness; but if, as Leigh Hunt tells in his tale of Abou-ben-Adam, those who love their neighbours well are first of those who love God, the task our fellow-labourer has taken up is second to no human duty. Many a peril and a bitter cross are in the path of the sanitary soldier. There are arrows of death flying around him, unseen. Minute enemies steal up from the standing pool, and through that opened door comes the fever breath of the poor child, gasping for pure air, where there is none. Men fight duels when insulted, or face a single enemy, in battle, when the blood is roused to mere animal heat; but he who exposes himself to feel what wretches feel, must do so by an impulse not common, and with a thought as noble as it is kind. We step out of our way to praise Mr. Godwin. We do so deliberately. We think it right now, while our true-hearted brother is doing well his chosen task, to tell him, from our heart, that there are many who, without even a knowledge of his person, honour him for his good intent and useful action. Better thus than reserve our praise for set occasions of 'silver' testimonial, or for empty words, to 'soothe the dull cold ear of death.'"